A Year of Cats and Dogs

A Year of Cats and Dogs

Margaret Hawkins

THE PERMANENT PRESS
Sag Harbor, NY 11963

For information, address:
The Permanent Press
4170 Noyac Road
Sag Harbor, NY 11963
www.thepermanentpress.com

Library of Congress Cataloging-in-Publication Data

Hawkins, Margaret—
    A year of cats and dogs / Margaret Hawkins.
        p. cm.
    ISBN-13: 978-1-57962-189-6 (hardcover : alk. paper)
    ISBN-10: 1-57962-189-9 (hardcover : alk. paper)
        1. Middle-aged women—Fiction. 2. Conduct of life—Fiction.
    I. Title.

PS3608.A89345Y43 2009
813'.6—dc22   2009026619

Printed in the United States of America.

For Fritz

AUTHOR'S NOTE

Chapter titles mirror those in the I Ching, *the Chinese book of changes. The* I Ching *is the three-thousand-year-old Taoist spiritual guide that recommends passive acceptance of and reflection on the lessons of the inner Sage to achieve prosperity and peace of mind. Each of the sixty-four chapter headings in this book corresponds to one of sixty-four possible coin throws, the process by which the* I Ching *is consulted. The version I used was* The I Ching *or* Book of Changes: A Guide to Life's Turning Points, *Brian Browne Walker's highly accessible translation published by St. Martin's Press in 1992.*

ACKNOWLEDGEMENTS

I owe a debt of gratitude to my agent, Jodie Rhodes, for believing in this book before anyone else even read it and to Martin and Judith Shepard, the editors and publishers of The Permanent Press, who took a risk on my odd invention. I'd also like to acknowledge the spirit of Max, the good dog who lived large and was my muse.

CHAPTER 1

Ch'ien / The Creative

If you are alert to the Creative,
you will meet with good fortune now.

In the morning the crows bear away the bodies of the mice my cat kills at night. He, Clement, leaves them whole in the center of the welcome mat, neatly delivered like a newspaper or a bottle of milk. Except for double pinpricks of blood on their necks, they are perfect. Once there was a bat so light I thought it was a cluster of dark leaves, another time a headless blue jay, then an opossum baby still damp and pinkly marsupial, with soft shut eyelids, the naked whip of his tail limp and still. But usually I find velvety gray mice with quiet faces and praying hands. I drink tea and watch the crows from the window after I shovel their small corpses onto the lawn.

Clement came to live here less than a year ago. It is his first spring with me, hunting season, and people who know these things tell me his gifts won't last, that they are a courtship ritual meant to win me over. But for now I enjoy them, though morbidly. I've learned to accept that his sweetness in the house is proportional to the murders he commits outside of it. Life in suburbia is not as dull as my city friends think. Or if it is, it is just the right kind of dull for me.

I live here alone now, in a house with a yard and a picket fence meant for four or two but not for one. Of course I am not truly alone because I live with animals. We are three, a woman, a dog and a cat.

I am forty-nine years old, heading for the big five-oh as my ex used to say. My name is Maryanne, a name made up of my two grandmothers' names combined in me like their genes are combined in my body and their mismatched china in my cupboard, china from which I serve my cat his Fancy Feast every day. This year I am the same age as my dog Bob if you count each of his seven years as seven. Bob and I have both slowed down some since we, my ex and I, picked him out at the animal shelter six and a half years ago, a hopeful Rottweiler puppy with a fighting scar on his open face. Since then he has grown gray around the muzzle while I get highlights three times a year. As for Clement the orange cat, I don't know his age. The people who left him here said they heard he was born in a drainpipe on Christmas Day but they didn't know the year. Depending on who tells the story we named him after either the small oranges that come at Christmas in a wooden crate or the great right fielder, for his ability to catch a rolled grape with one paw.

The thing about living with animals is you're never alone. When your partner your sweetie your main squeeze your baby your heart your one your only your love your life your husband your wife moves out you think you'll go crazy or at least be lonely and you do and you are at first but then mostly you're not. The animals close in around you, good company that keeps you busy and warm in bed, and they are never critical. Sometimes they leave muddy footprints on the toilet seat or wake you up in the middle of the night with their small insistent demands: I'm hungry, please fill my bowl. Please, may I go out now? I think I smell a skunk and I'd like to try to kill it. Or, I'm cold. Please, dear, would you move over so I may get in? And may I please bring this ham bone I found in the alley also? But who could care about those things. You never mind because they so clearly like you, love you, even, if you believe in that sort of thing.

That was the problem with Phillip. So often he didn't seem to, like me that is, or didn't seem to know if he did or not and was taking his time to think it over very carefully, ten years, to be exact, to figure it out, as if he didn't want to go on record as having made a mistake. And maybe it was easier for me that way too, never having to feel backed into a corner, never having to make a choice. We always left a way out and finally he took it. When he moved out it was almost a relief that he'd finally decided. At least I didn't have to wonder anymore what to call him: Lover? Boyfriend? Partner? Mate? Friend? At least now there was an exact word for what he was: ex.

When Phillip first moved out he said it was temporary. His company needed him in Seattle and he'd be back in six months. We both only half believed it. But it was an easy fiction to go along with because in a way you could say he had everything to return to: his clothes in the closet, those silk-lined cashmere blazers on padded hangers, lined up by color, his long-dead mother's picture in a silver frame on the mantle, his sister's phone number on speed dial, his brand of beer—a high-priced, hard-to-find variety of ale made by Belgian monks, still in the refrigerator—the animals. I wondered how he could leave them, Clement and Bob, but he just took the things he wanted and left the rest, including me.

There is a picture of us together taken not long before he moved out. It used to hang on the refrigerator, affixed with a magnet in the shape of a bone. I kept it there until it was too painful to look at and then I took it down and shoved it into his copy of *The Joy of Cooking*, which I'd given him one year for his birthday and which he'd left behind. I stuck the picture between the pages where the recipe for liver pâté was. I made it every Christmas and he liked it, though if he'd known where the recipe came from he wouldn't have. The picture was taken by a friend at a dinner party we'd given and it shows us in the kitchen posed in front of our Viking stove holding platters of food we were about to carry to the table. Phillip stands a head taller than me, in his usual elegant posture, broad shoulders relaxed, black turtleneck and short-cropped black curly hair flecked with gray framing his milky white face. Intense blue eyes, long black lashes. I can't tell what else he's wearing, probably black jeans that fit just so. He smiles remotely, his finely contoured lips curving in a satisfied way that makes handsome dents on either side of his mouth. He holds a platter of garlic noodles piled high with broiled shrimp and artistically tossed with fresh Vietnamese basil. He looks like he thinks he is alone. But he is not. Next to him stands a flushed, round-faced, round-shouldered woman with a lopsided smile wearing smudged red lipstick. She leans toward him, looking slightly drunk and overly pink in the face, her straight shoulder-length flyaway hair a nondescript color that might once have been light brown but was now streaked blond over gray. She is me. I also wear a black turtleneck and although I am average in my height and appearance, next to Phillip I look small, plain, squat and lumpy, like a smitten tourist posing with an affable celebrity, pleased to have my picture snapped before he's whisked off to his next engagement. I hold a plate of skewered vegetable kabobs fresh off the grill. Phillip won't let me near the shrimp.

At first he came back on weekends, then once a month and then not at all. In the end he didn't seem to miss any of it much, just moved on, and part of me admired his ability to let go, to shed us. I came across a tuft of his hair stuck to a blanket once and another time I found a pair of paint-stained pants in a corner of the basement months after he'd gone as if he'd just stepped out of them. It wasn't clear if he'd meant to leave them for me to dispose of or had just forgotten to take them. When I checked the pockets I found exactly one personal item: an old wine cork, a token of some dinner past, maybe even the last one. It's just him that's gone and it took me awhile to notice he wasn't coming back. Phillip, of course, had met someone else.

CHAPTER 2

K'un / The Receptive

Bear with things as the earth bears with us:
By yielding, by accepting, by nourishing.

We talked one night, on one of his weekend visits home, about the possibility of staying together but loosely. Or he talked about it. We'd still be a couple here, he said. No big deal and I could start dating if I liked, although, he pointed out, I shouldn't do it just out of spite. He explained the plan over a dinner of roast duck, red cabbage and wild rice he'd spent all Saturday cooking. He'd brought a special jar of orange sauce all the way from Seattle, bubble-wrapped in his overnight bag, to pour over the duck in the last stages of cooking. He'd obviously made this particular version of duck before, though I'd never tasted it, and seemed to be in the process of perfecting the recipe. For him, he said, it was like having two pets: you loved them both in different ways. He said this as we ate and I supposed it made sense but I couldn't finish my duck breast. He was insulted that I didn't eat because he'd made it crispy just the way I liked it.

The next day he flew back and after that we didn't talk for a long time. The day I realized he was really gone I threw the *I Ching* and got the fifth hexagram, *Hsü/Waiting: To wait with a proper attitude invites the assistance of the Higher Power.* For the first line I threw a nine so I read the instructions for that, which said: *A challenge lies ahead. Ready yourself by deepening the stillness within.*

I took the advice to heart. I could do that, I thought, and I was glad that at least according to one system of philosophy I didn't have to take action. I interpreted it to mean I didn't have to tell any friends who would give me advice to the contrary. Instead I set about trying to deepen the stillness within. It wasn't difficult. For one thing I now had permission to take long naps.

But the habits of couple-hood die hard. For awhile it was like living in a picture that had a hole cut out of it in the shape of Phillip with everything the same except for his absence. I didn't fill the hole, I just sewed up the frayed edges and worked around it, an arrangement that made the hole very important.

I kept everything as it had been. I still cooked dinner every night though at first I couldn't eat and gave it all to Bob. Then I couldn't stop eating. I repeated all our old habits but distorted them to break Phillip's rules. I ate all the forbidden foods, the low-rent foods I craved, which Phillip had outlawed: canned soup, fish sticks, macaroni and cheese, tuna casserole with potato chips. I came home from work every night, took a nap and then made enough dinner for two and what I couldn't finish Bob did. I stayed on my side of the garage and my side of the bed and Bob took over the other half, sleeping with his head on Phillip's pillow with his back to me and his legs sticking straight out like a stout barrel-chested man in a black fur coat, passing gas occasionally and twitching in his sleep. Now that Phillip was gone Bob was more protective than ever. Clement didn't seem affected at all. Supervising us was just his part-time job, after his main vocations of hunting and sleeping. Being alone but not alone was strange at first but not the end of the world in the way it would have seemed if I had known from the beginning that I was being left for good. Adapt and overcome, as the Marines say; you get used to anything.

I started wearing Phillip's clothes and when they got dirty, instead of washing them, I threw them out, one item at a time, experiencing a guilty thrill every time I dumped one of his pricey garments into the trash. I used his cashmere scarf to dry the dog after a walk in the rain, and when it caught on his toenails and tore, I threw that out too. It felt good to get rid of things. I started to fantasize about culling my life: selling the house, quitting my job, joining the Peace Corps but only if they let me take along the animals, even about other men, though I didn't have the energy for that. I concentrated on throwing things out.

As time went on I fantasized more and more about quitting my job. I felt I'd earned the right to let things go. I wanted to embrace entropy, to stop working so hard at keeping things up. I wanted to go AWOL from the productive world I'd so long been a part of. It was my turn to be irresponsible, I reasoned. I gave myself permission to not wipe up the yogurt on the counter, not open the mail, not keep my hair appointment, not answer the phone, not make the bed, not put away the laundry. Not do the laundry. Or the dishes or the bills or my hair. For the first time I considered the possibility of skipping holidays altogether, wearing my clothes inside out, going into debt and growing really fat. One didn't die of these things, usually, one just went downhill slowly. Wasn't that what aging was? It might be fun, I thought, more fun at least than what I had been doing which amounted to paying the bills on time and going to bed early. The clearer it became that Phillip wasn't coming back the more I wanted to hurry up and let things fall apart, just to see what would happen.

CHAPTER 3

Chun / Difficulty at the Beginning

If we persevere a great success is at hand.

I worked for Keepsake Cottage, a thriving collectibles company that occupied a dumpy three-story office building wedged between a used car lot and a downscale shopping mall on a commercial strip in a treeless suburb north of Chicago. We sold those little decorative objects advertised in the Sunday newspaper, ready-made for collecting from nearly indestructible materials, as if there weren't already enough little lumps of resin with a half-life of a million years sitting on shelves around the world. We made plates, figurines, revolving ceramic Christmas trees, nightlights printed with Bible verses, musical charm bracelets, talking snow globes, dancing Russian dolls, picture frames in the shape of dogs, candy dishes equipped with motion detectors that played the Moonlight Sonata when you filled them with chocolate.

People called them chatchkes, dust catchers, worthless junk, and I did too at first. At first it seemed funny and a little immoral but after a while less so especially when they promoted me to Keepsake Collector Liaison and it became my job to visit customers in their homes and interview them about what they liked. I always went in the morning and brought a Bisquick crumb cake, which I made myself the night before. It put them at ease, and as we sat at their kitchen tables drinking instant decaf and looking at scrapbooks full of pictures of their dead pets they told me with tears in their eyes how happy their collections made them. That's when my job stopped being funny and took on a weird gravity, when I stopped being sure it was a worthless thing to do.

Pretty soon, though, the vice president of Psychological Research, Motivation and Marketing eliminated my position. I'd found out everything he wanted to know, even our customers' favorite color. It was purple. After that I was given a raise and moved to product development. Ten years later I was still there; it paid the bills.

The company's mission statement said its purpose was to bring joy and happiness to its customers. We all laughed about that. It forgot to mention the part about making lots of money for the suited ones who ran the place. But I had to admit that if avarice fueled the business, joy was at least a by-product. These little objects, in addition to making a few people rich, did appear to make a lot of others happy. Or at least they kept lonely people company and maybe that was almost the same thing.

My job title, after I was promoted, was Keepsake Conceptualizer for Sentiments and Social Expressions. We had a form to fill out when we presented new ideas to the Vice President of Innovation and Imagination that required us to identify the joy factor for each new product. When I presented a new idea for resin puppy figurines hiding in slippers and boots, each of which was to contain a sound chip that played an endearing melody such as "How Much is that Doggie in the Window?" I was required to write "love of dogs" on the line labeled JF. If it was a cat sleeping in a hat, I wrote "love of cats," and then "love of hats," just to be sure. Later, after much deliberation, they changed the title of that line from "joy factor" to "bliss quotient" but it meant the same thing. If you came up with a product with a high enough bliss quotient you got a bonus check at the end of the year for one hundred dollars and a gift certificate for one free lunch in the company cafeteria.

I worked on cat clocks that meowed every hour on the hour, dog clocks that wagged their tails, little resin angels that twirled around and held banners that said things like a mother's love is a gift from above, plates with verses on them about the joys of home and friendship, resin figurines of Jesus and Elvis that were lit from within by glowing red hearts, stained glass window ornaments featuring chirping songbirds and howling wolves and photo frames decaled with poems about grieving for dead relatives. Sometimes I wrote the poems. Sometimes I sat in my beige cubicle drinking green tea and reading the Bible looking for verses that went well with cats and dogs, angels or eagles. After I exhausted the obvious choices—Matthew 7:7 "Knock and the door shall be opened unto you" printed on an angel-shaped doorknocker was an early success—I looked for hidden gems. More than once I pitched them Song of Solomon 8:6, "Love is strong as death," for a heart-shaped pet gravestone but they didn't like that. They said it sounded harsh, though to my ear it was hopeful.

But after Phillip moved out it was harder than ever to find my job fulfilling, let alone funny. Sometimes I just sat at my desk and stared at the phone, wishing I could call Bob and see how he was. When I couldn't stand that anymore I slipped out a side door and drove to the forest preserve, passing miles of strip malls and fast food restaurants on my way. There I walked around the man-made pond, averting my eyes from the pale flesh of lovers in the bushes, and fed the ducks until one day a ranger told me bread would expand in their throats and make them choke and die. Then I drove back to the office and tried to write more poems.

It was not my job to actually sculpt or paint anything—I didn't make things, I developed them, which meant I came up with ideas and hired other people to do the actual making. I sent my concepts to freelance artists in small towns around the country, sweet-sounding women in Oklahoma and Arkansas who called me honey and spoke warmly to me on the phone in slow, syrupy accents and didn't charge much money. Then I sent their drawings to factories in China where anonymous sculptors with small hands earning small wages fashioned pretty figures out of their clumsy sketches.

One way or the other the products I worked on were all about love: love of pets, love of Jesus, love of roses, love of panda bears, love of the U.S. Marines, love of Elvis, love of family. But I was tired of love. Love suddenly seemed like a frayed coat I'd out-grown, or a club I'd been voted out of. It seemed like an outdated, Pollyannaish concept, like putting all your pocket change in a piggy bank every night or drinking eight glasses of water a day. All those years you had to do it and then suddenly you didn't anymore and it turned out not to matter as much as everyone had told you it did. In fact it didn't matter at all. Not that I didn't love the animals, Bob and Clement, or even Phillip in a nostalgic, sick kind of way, and probably lots of other people and places and ideas and entities and God almighty him or herself, occasionally. But after ten years at the company and with Phillip, I was not even very good at it any more, the job or love. I'd lost track of what love was supposed to be, forgotten what you were supposed to do once you were afflicted with it. Other than feeding the animals and tending to their needs I could not think of what it meant.

CHAPTER 4

Mêng / Youthful Folly

*Even the foolish can attain wisdom
by modestly following the Sage.*

Anticipating what I was about to do but not quite ready to admit it, I walked into a bank on my lunch hour one day and took out a line of credit on my house. Let me say here that I owned it. I suppose the fact that Phillip didn't want the entanglement of joint ownership should have been a sign, but when it came time to take action on my own it did make things easier. The financial consultant, a nervous young man in a blue polo shirt with earnest dark eyes and wearing a nametag that said Steve M. Horvath, Jr. said I had the highest FICO score he'd ever seen. I didn't know what a FICO score was. I'd just been to the veterinarian with Bob a few days before and thought he'd said fecal score and didn't reply. When he explained, all I could figure was this was because I didn't like to shop and always paid my bills. These didn't seem like particularly distinguishing features but resulted in my being authorized to borrow a great deal of money at a record low interest rate.

Steve M. Horvath, Jr. checked and double-checked that I was the only signer of the mortgage. Yes I said it's only me. He looked dubious but I pretended not to notice. I didn't want to tell him the details, about how I bought the house, not we, or about how the first night we slept on the floor in front of the fireplace and how we planted a lilac bush in the front yard the first spring we lived there and daisies and tomatoes in the back yard and that the tomatoes were mealy and tasteless and mostly eaten by marauding deer. I didn't tell him that as soon as we combined our households Phillip made me throw out all my wineglasses and most of my furniture. I didn't tell him how we took three rolls of pictures of the house the first time it snowed or that the first Christmas we bought two Christmas trees and decorated them separately because Phillip disapproved of my ornaments. I didn't tell him that the other members of the we I referred to when describing my current household were all four-legged. I didn't fill him in on Bob's sleeping habits or Clement's murderous gifts let alone on Phillip's comings and goings and when he saw on his computer screen that indeed I was the sole owner he sneaked one last look at me over the rim of his aviator glasses and then gave up trying to figure me out. He shook my hand and congratulated me and I was free to go forth and borrow.

I quit my job two weeks later. I was hard pressed to explain when my boss asked why. Most people leave for a better job, or at least for a plan, but I had neither. I said I was going to freelance, hardly probable given my passionless job performance—how could I do this work on my own if I couldn't do it under pressure of meetings, reviews, presentations and threats—but she took me at my word and said she'd be calling me for more of those great poems. On the last day my work friends took me to lunch at an Indian restaurant where we ate chicken curry with saffron rice and drank Maharaja beer and then it was over.

CHAPTER 5

Hsü / Waiting (Nourishment)

To wait with a proper attitude
invites the assistance of the Higher Power.

"Follow your passion," my friend Donna said when I told her I'd given notice and didn't know what to do next. I was embarrassed to tell her I didn't think I had one. Donna was one of those people who liked to give what she believed to be helpful advice to lost souls and though we were old friends sometimes I suspected she liked me mainly as a fix-up project.

The first day I didn't have to go to work I spent the morning walking Bob, drinking tea and shopping for groceries. In the afternoon I made chicken soup. Then I read a magazine, turned off the soup and took a nap before dinner. I thought I'd be euphoric but all I felt was numb and sad. The second day I ate the soup for breakfast, walked Bob, read another magazine and took another nap. Here's how I made the soup. It's the uninspired, quickie, depressed person's version; in a joyous mood I would have done more. I would have started earlier in the morning, using dried beans instead of canned ones and made my own stock from a whole chicken and a bunch of celery, leaves and all. Still, this version is pretty good, though you might find it bland:

Quitting Your Job and Vowing to be Frugal Stew: Chicken Soup for the Sad

In a big pot, sauté a couple of chicken breasts and a few drumsticks in olive oil. You can fry up some bacon in the pot too at this point if you want although I didn't because I was feeling Spartan that day, having just quit my job. If you do add bacon make sure that it's crisp and broken into pieces before you add liquid.

Add a medium-sized finely chopped onion to the olive oil and chicken fat. When the onion is transparent or nearly so add minced garlic, two or three cloves to taste, but turn the heat way down immediately and make sure it doesn't burn or even brown. The important thing to remember here and anytime you're making a sauce or soup that uses both onion and garlic is this: the more you cook onion the sweeter it gets but garlic is just the opposite. If you burn it, it becomes bitter and is ruined.

I poured a glass of wine and started to think about this. It seemed like an important insight. People were this way too, I thought, either garlic or onion. Some people, under heat, get sweeter; trouble, stress, hardship warms them, makes them more human and breaks down the rough edges. Others just grow bitter.

For a minute or two I imagined this insight would be my financial salvation. For the first time since I'd begun to entertain the notion of quitting my job a vision of a prosperous future spooled out in front of me. I imagined an inspirational lecture tour, saw myself traveling across the country in fitted pantsuits, speaking on the subject of Onion or Garlic: Which One Are You? But it was a short-lived fantasy. I couldn't see myself mounting a campaign against the moral character of garlic, which is what it came down to, since I liked garlic and especially since I knew I was more garlic than onion, myself. I set my wine down and returned to the soup.

Add 2 cans chicken stock or 4 cubes of chicken bouillon and about 4 cups of water. Add 4 or 5 skinned red potatoes, chopped finely. Simmer them awhile until they're soft before you add other vegetables. They should crumble when you poke them with a fork.

Add half a cabbage, chopped, 3 or 4 chopped carrots, some celery with the leaves on and whatever other vegetables you have around. I rummaged around in the dingy plastic drawer in my refrigerator and came up with a quarter head of cauliflower, half a zucchini and some dried-up parsley that had been there for months. They made adequate additions.

Add spices—herbes de Provence are good or, on a budget, just rosemary—but use whatever you have and like. And pepper of course, lots. Skip the salt if you're using bouillon; it's already too salty.

Simmer a couple of hours and then take out the chicken skin and the bones as they come apart from the meat. Cool the skin and feed it to the dog.

At this point I usually add wine. I pour the wine into a glass first and then drink about half and pour the rest into the pot, wishing cheers to the soup. Then I repeat. When I do this the soup assumes the role of a companion and collaborator, albeit one who will ultimately be eaten. We share a drink, the soup and I, toasting the progress of the meal. I read somewhere once about the Zen practice of pouring wine onto the roots of pine trees on special occasions and always thought it was a good idea although I've yet to try it.

Add a can or two of white beans toward the end, making sure they boil but briefly. Only add the beans at the beginning if they are dry. Canned beans get too soft when you cook them too long and finally they completely dissolve leaving nothing but empty skins, which float depressingly around in the soup like dead insect wings. Beware of this; sorrow and soup don't mix well.

I recommend butter beans because they are big and pale, flat and beautiful, like stones in a riverbed. They look good in a soup and I like how the name sounds: butter beans. They are the color of vanilla, velvety when you bite down, and true to their name, they taste like butter.

You can serve the soup for 2, if you have a friend, in wide shallow bowls. Give each person an intact but falling-apart skinless chicken breast, which looks elegant especially with the big butter beans in the mixture and if you sprinkle cracked pepper and fresh parsley on top. Or if you're alone, like me, just shred the chicken into the soup. Take out the bones if you do this but of course don't give those to your dog.

CHAPTER 6

Sung / Conflict

*The proper response to conflict, whether it lies within
or without us, is disengagement.*

I knew the neighbors thought I was odd. My being home all the time just made it worse. I didn't look busy enough to them. After a few weeks Lisa slowed down her enormous silver SUV alongside me one day as I was walking Bob and called out, as if I'd asked, "You should have a baby!" Apparently she hadn't noticed Phillip was gone. Thinking fast I called back in what I intended to be a cheerful, breezy way, "I'm too old!" and then smiled as ingratiatingly as I could. I hoped it was enough to stop the subject, offering my age up as a kind of sacrifice. If I admitted to being old maybe she would feel I had suffered enough and would leave me alone. She shook her head and gunned the engine, in a hurry to get to her pottery class. She was the busy-ness police and I'd just been given a warning.

What happens when nothing happens I wondered. Can you live the whole second half of your life just walking the dog and living on savings, with no plan and nothing to do? Did life need a plot or could it just be? It seemed that just living was already enough to do, was exhausting in fact, all this eating, cleaning up, taking Bob on his walks, tending to Clement's litter box. I was tired of being busy.

But there was living and then there was making a living. I figured I'd saved enough to go a year without work if I was careful, six months if I lived exactly as I had been living, minus Phillip. Phillip made money and liked to spend it but with him gone I could turn down the thermostat, drink cheap wine and eat Ramen noodles for dinner. I could last a long time.

And there was the occasional job. Despite my lackluster business skills I had already lined up a freelance assignment from my old boss to write a poem to be called "For the Luv o' Puppies: Eight Days a Week." The idea was that the love of puppies exceeds what could be contained in a mere seven days so I was to write a verse for each day and then an eighth-day finale.

In addition to work to keep me busy, there was my social life which by now, since I was unwilling to admit to anyone that Phillip had left, had telescoped down to dog-walking sessions with Donna and weekly visits from my eighty-eight-year-old father who came like clockwork every week for Sunday dinner, driving the half hour from his house in Niles in his immaculate seventeen-year-old Ford Escort. I worried about him on the road and offered to go to his house but he said no he preferred to come to mine. He liked to drive he said and he liked to see the animals and when he came to my place it meant that I cooked and washed the dishes. He missed seeing Phillip of course but we had a tacit agreement to act as if he was coming back, a claim that he politely pretended to believe. When he asked for details I made up stories about what I imagined Phillip was up to, hiking, traveling on business, negotiating deals, and then I'd convey his good wishes as if we'd just spoken that morning and my father would convey his own heartily back.

My father accepted these stories unquestioningly and without much interest. There'd been other boyfriends, a long engagement even, and he'd given up expecting me to marry any of them, let alone procreate. He'd stopped asking fifteen years ago what he should do with the matching child-sized desk and dresser in the basement which apparently he'd been saving to pass on to any offspring of mine or my older sister's, and finally gave them away to a pretty neighbor who was pregnant with her fourth. The day I noticed they were gone from his basement was the day I knew I was not going to have children. I couldn't bring myself to discuss these matters with him but I did tell him I'd quit my job. I said that within a week of giving notice I was nearly overwhelmed with the work pouring into my freelance business, a story that I think he believed because he couldn't imagine I'd be foolish enough to quit for nothing. I couldn't tell him the truth; he'd think I was hitting him up for money.

"So how's business?" he'd say after he'd settled himself down into a kitchen chair with excruciating slowness, eyeing the cheese assortment I'd set out for him. He ignored my answer as he studied the cheeses. "What's this? What are these flecks?" he asked fiercely, pronouncing the word with great precision while holding up a slice of jalapeño pepper jack balanced on my grandmother's sterling butter knife, his rheumy blue eyes inspecting it suspiciously. "Hot pepper cheese, Dad," I'd shout from the sink where I was chopping vegetables. He was a little hard of hearing, nothing extreme but enough that I knew if I wanted to really converse I'd better speak up and all I had to do to insult and exclude him was to use my normal voice.

He upended the cheese chunk onto a slightly stale Ritz cracker and popped it into his mouth. A dreamy look crept into his eyes. "Tasty," he said, nodding and chewing very slowly.

He was missing teeth and those he did have were loose, so I planned Sunday dinners around the chewability of the food: soups, stews, meat loaf, fish, mashed potatoes. Ice cream, angel food cake, banana splits for dessert. Cheese and martinis as a first course were mandatory while steaks and raw salads were out of the question. Anything too coarse was passed to Bob under the table and choice bits that were soft enough but too much for my father's diminishing appetite were wrapped in a napkin and carried home in his shirt pocket, to be mashed into his oatmeal and eaten, slowly, for breakfast the next day.

CHAPTER 7

Shih / The Army

*In times of war it is desirable to be led by
a cautious and humane general.*

I developed a routine. I got up in the dark to walk Bob, less likely at that hour to encounter any one of a cast of characters at the park this early in the morning. There was Mike with his standard poodle, Sven, who always steered the conversation to something vaguely sexual, and there was Nancy whose dachshund Johnny (Cash) liked for Bob to urinate on him. There was Aaron who sang in Hebrew to his Weimaraner and Don the milkman who delivered upscale dairy products and waited in the park two mornings a week until it was time to make his deliveries; he liked to chat about recipes. I liked these people and hoped our friendships could survive my moratorium on sociability. But I didn't feel like explaining why no one had seen Phillip in months or what I was up to, which in fact I didn't know. So far I didn't seem to be up to anything.

When I got home I took a bath. The animals came to join me. They trotted down the hall together at the first sound of the water roaring into the tub, then waited outside the bathroom door until I got in, Bob, eager and relaxed from his morning outing, and Clement in his perpetual state of meditative alertness. As soon as I settled into the water Bob bumped the door open with his nose and they rushed in, vying for position, Bob shouldering Clement out the way, Clement leaping onto the toilet and then the sink, asserting his superior vertical mobility against Bob's greater mass. Finally both took their positions, the dog alongside the tub and the cat poised on its rim, hanging his face down into the steam, and, together, they drank. I lay half submerged, watching them lap up the soapy water in the weak morning light, careful not to splash Clement by shampooing too violently. It was usually the best part of my day.

Sometimes I considered whether this was too weird, whether I took some kind of perverse sexual thrill in appearing naked in front of my male pets. My breasts bobbed out of the water just inches from my cat's darting tongue but did this give me sexual pleasure? It did not, though I almost wished it did. If I were really serious about going off the deep end this would be a good start. But the pleasure was more companionable, a continuation of our pacific three-way friendship. And frankly they didn't seem interested in me that way. No one did.

I found this was exactly how I wanted to spend my time. I knew my high-achieving friends, most of whom I'd avoided for months, would find my life shockingly empty if I told them what I was doing. But sometimes I felt fulfilled or at least oddly content. Some days I even took two baths, one in the evening, just to repeat the ritual, though the animals only drank from the tub in the morning.

CHAPTER 8

Pi / Holding Together (Union)

Seek union with others and with the Sage.

Once a week, sometimes more, I drove to Petsmart to buy supplies. I didn't need to go that often but it was a comforting routine, anonymous and undemanding. I'd put Bob on his leash and walk up and down the aisles pushing a cart, filling it with bargains, little cans of savory-sounding cat food and big bags of dog food or low-priced treats. Something was always happening there. Rescue groups were trying to place three-legged German shepherds in good homes and puppies were being taught to run through plastic tunnels on command. Hamsters ran circles on wheels in glass cages and big birds with colorful beaks croaked non sequiturs. Mostly I'd watch the dogs being groomed behind a big plate glass window. They stood on high tables, shivering, their leashes hooked up to posts to keep them still while the groomers stood alongside, intent on their combing and buzz-cutting chores.

Usually the grooming room was full of small white dogs with alert intelligent faces and rust-colored, moon-shaped stains under their eyes, as if they'd been crying coffee and blood. After the grooming was done a little kerchief was tied around the dog's neck, red in the winter, yellow in the spring. When the owners came to collect them the dogs rushed out, fragrant and smooth, wagging from the neck down, as relieved to be released as kindergartners sprung from school at lunch.

Sometimes bigger dogs stood on the tables. One day I saw a shivering golden retriever, white with age around the muzzle, with his tail pressed firmly against his anus and curling between his legs as he eyed the buzzing thing that moved around his head.

I tried to send him calming thoughts through the thick glass and it seemed to me his shivering stopped.

Then I visited the orphan cat room. Mostly the cats slept in piles, looking indifferent to their circumstances, not seeming to mind the acrid smell and the institutional surroundings, and apparently not that interested in going home with anyone. In fact they seemed pleased to be there, lying around, hanging out. That's what Clement did when he was inside, he lay around. One hour on the couch, sleeping in a circle with his head tucked into the crook in front of his back legs, then a half hour on the dining room chair. Then to bed for a really long nap. Sometimes he'd crawl inside a brown paper grocery bag left on the floor and seemed to enjoy the rustling sounds he made while he situated himself but then he settled, peering out at me if I looked in. Or he climbed into my lap when I watched TV, kneading the soft flesh there as if walking on some slow motion treadmill, purring loudly and staring up at me intently. Then, his bed made on me, he'd lie down and fall asleep. That was all he did, inside at least, except for eating and a little prancing across the kitchen table to sniff a banana or bat at a rubber band. When he felt the urge he'd levitate onto the kitchen counter then float over to his bowl and munch studiously on kibble, his whole body curved over the project, always leaving a few morsels behind. Was he leaving the remains for a leaner time? It didn't seem to make sense. Perhaps Clement was just a thrifty eccentric, like my father. After he ate he sat patiently at the door like a man waiting for a train, and when I opened it he rushed out and hustled into the bushes, off on his daily rounds of killing.

Watching the animals calmed me. It made me feel justified in not doing much myself. Every morning I threw the *I Ching* and often I got the Waiting hexagram, reassuring me that deepening the stillness within was still the right way to go. If anyone asked what I was up to I thought I might try to explain about the *I Ching* and the cats. And the dogs. Bob was the same as Clement. Though he followed me when I moved around, when I settled somewhere in the house he seemed happy just to lie there next to me. Or to go back to bed as I often did when I couldn't think of the next thing to do. I imagined he might be thinking, remembering things he enjoyed or looking forward to some future pleasure or even worrying about some troubling concern. But it also seemed possible he was doing nothing of the kind, that unlike me he truly lived in the present.

He'd lie on his side on the couch, his thick body like a black barrel and his head lolling off to the side so that the bumpy black flesh around his mouth hung straight down. His eyes were hooded and red, his unfocused gaze aimed at a window where passed occasional specimens of suburban wildlife: a rabbit, occasionally a deer, a squirrel, a dog walker, a jogger, or Clement when he was on the prowl. Only the daily threat of the mailman roused him and not even every time.

All these animals can't be wrong, I thought. If I can arrange to pay the bills somehow, why can't I spend the rest of my time being as still as they are?

CHAPTER 9

Hsiao Ch'u / The Taming Power of the Small

You are temporarily restrained.
It is a time for taking small steps.

Three weeks into my ill-considered retirement, I was sitting at my computer at ten o'clock on a Wednesday morning immersed in my second freelance assignment. I was writing a patriotic song lyric roughly fashioned after Woody Guthrie's "This Land Is Your Land," which was to appear on the back of a flag-draped angel's wing, when the doorbell rang. It was Diane, my neighbor from down the block, holding two-year-old Gloria on her hip and Gregoire, an epileptic collie, on a leash. The baby looked hot in her coat. Dark wisps of hair were matted to her chocolaty skin and a salty-looking yellow crumb was loosely stuck to the dark rose globe of her cheek. She smelled humid and sweet.

Diane was in her usual state of agitation. "I am so glad you answered the door," she said, referring offhandedly and for the first time to the fact that sometimes I didn't and just sat frozen at my desk and let the doorbell ring. I wondered how she knew. "Is there any way you could possibly take Gregoire for a few days." It wasn't a question. "We just got the call from the agency and the baby is ready for us to pick up. But we have to go before the government changes its mind." Bob was behind me trying to muscle his way past my legs and out the door to grab Gregoire by the big glamorous ruff of fur around his neck while I was still half humming the song lyric in my head. "This flag is your flag this flag is my flag, from the hands of Betsy Ross to the foot to the old rugged cross." I was wondering if it was too much. Something was off.

"Sure" I said, thinking I could fix the meter but worrying if maybe it was the images that didn't work. I wanted to keep the rhyme though. Diane was in the house now, unclipping Gregoire's leash and brushing crumbs from Gloria's cheek. They were adopting their third South American baby, a process that required a lot of travel, and the more children they got the more time Gregoire spent with us.

"Bop!" said Gloria, who was wearing a diaper and a purple T-shirt with a smiley face on it that crept up her belly. She swayed in her perch on Diane's hip as she waved her little pink-palmed hands in the air over Bob who now had a firm grip on Gregoire's hugely fluffy coat and was systematically ripping out mouthfuls of it.

"You should know he had a seizure last week. He puked beforehand though so if that happens you'll know it's coming and then he just lies down and moans a little and drools; but then afterward you have to reassure him and pet him, maybe lie down with him. And give him water." Gregoire was now standing on his hind legs and had his narrow opossum-like snout affixed to Bob's thick neck while Bob continued to pull out mouthfuls of Gregoire's spectacular collie coat. They danced in a circle, growling in a deep satisfied way, each holding the other upright at the throat.

"Bop's killing Greggor, Mom," Gloria reported somberly.

"They're just playing honey," Diane said, smoothing the baby's hair. "Listen, the cab's coming at four this afternoon and I've got to pack so I've got to go but thank you so much." Then they were gone, rushing down my front path with Gloria's head twisting around like an owl's to watch as the dogs and I receded behind her. She waved.

CHAPTER 10

Lü / Treading (Conduct)

Lasting progress is won through quiet self-discipline.

For a while I thought he'd come back. I said I didn't want him to but sometimes I did. Sometimes at night I imagined he would be dropped off by a cab in the dark, let himself in the back door and climb into bed with me so that when we woke up in the morning it would all be back to where it was before he left. Once about a month after I quit my job I was home sitting at the kitchen table in the morning when I heard a knock on the front door. I ran to the door sure it was him, stopping only to rearrange my hair in the reflection in the window of the microwave oven. But when I got to the door no one was there. I never figured out what happened. I was sure I'd heard the knock.

I started to believe it was him, sending a telepathic knock, expressing the desire to come back, if only for a moment, a desire that didn't last long enough for him to get up and make a phone call and go to the airport but still an instant of desire which traveled through space and time and manifested itself in a weak but audible presence at my door.

That was about the time I started to believe I was getting all kinds of messages. My dead mother, for instance, seemed to be reminding me to be kinder to my father by dropping pots on my foot when I entertained unforgiving thoughts about him as I unloaded the dishwasher, a phenomenon that seemed particularly supernatural since she never would have cared about that when she was alive. I had dreams of dead friends and relatives who seemed to be trying to tell me things I could never remember or which didn't make sense when I awoke. "Draw the pickle," advised my childhood friend Dawn who'd died in a porch collapse at a party in college, "round up the crayons." They were puzzles, poems that spoke to me. I believed in them but I didn't know what they meant. And especially, and more cogently, I began to receive messages from animals.

My own animals were always communicating with me of course, sending clear directives about food and water or wanting to go outside to sniff or kill or urinate. But now there were messages from the animals at the pet shop or the ones sitting in windows as I passed them on my walks with Bob. Sometimes I'd experiment and send a message back. "Hi. Quiet down," I'd say to them in my mind, "stop barking, everything is OK."

It seemed to work as long as the message I sent back was true; if I lied it didn't go through. "Everything is OK" didn't calm the dog that was about to be nicked by the groomer's razor. I had to word my reassurances carefully, editing out all lies. But sometimes I could be helpful. When I'd see a bird trapped behind an upper window of an empty house marked for demolition, flinging itself against the light, I'd send it a message telling it to stop, go back through whatever opening it had entered. And the bird would stop flinging itself against the window and disappear. I could only hope it found its way out the back door.

Around that time I saw Deepak Chopra on the Larry King Show. He looked handsomely dissolute with dark circles under his eyes and he was wearing a collarless shirt. We were all spiritual beings having a human experience, he said, looking seductively at Larry. I agreed but I wished he would have taken it further. My impression was that Bob and Clement and the neighborhood birds were spiritual beings having canine, feline and avian experiences, respectively. And now here was Gregoire; my house was full of spirit.

CHAPTER 11

T'ai / Peace

Heaven exists on earth for those who maintain
correct thoughts and actions.

When I run into people from my old job they ask me about my pets. It's awkward because I don't think of Bob and Clement as pets exactly but as beloved companions, honored associates, esteemed friends and colleagues. I feel embarrassed when I am asked this question. Seeing my animals as only pets trivializes our relationship and makes my involvement with them seem frivolous and merely eccentric and when people think that this trivial relationship is the only subject I am comfortable talking about that makes me seem odd and sad. Though they are right in one sense; it is the only subject I am comfortable talking about.

When they ask about Phillip I can feel my face freeze and I can't think of anything to say. He's well, he likes his job, I say, smiling falsely. Yes he's still in Seattle, too busy to come home this weekend. They can hear the quotation marks in my voice around the word home. For a while people extended dinner invitations as in "next time he's home we should all get together" and then they stopped because we never set it up because he never came home. Home wasn't home anymore. Then there was work. People kept asking what I was doing now but I didn't have an answer for that either and my weirdly sincere attempts at explaining sounded like lies. I didn't want to talk about any of it because I didn't want to hear what people had to say.

Take my friend Miriam, who was always a little suspicious of the animal situation in my house anyway. She kept hinting she thought Phillip had left because of them, even before I knew he'd left. "You know I love Jingle," she'd said once, referring to her ill-tempered Persian cat, and making the kind of eye contact that meant she meant something deeper, "but I put him on the floor when Jimmy wants to cuddle." She meant sex. She thought I put Bob between Phillip and me in bed but the fact is that, until Phillip moved out, Bob slept on the floor at the foot of the bed, not in-between us. Ever since she'd taken a seminar at the Kinsey Institute Miriam was convinced my real love affair was with Bob. She couldn't understand I could be this involved with him and Clement without having sex with them.

And Miriam has a cat. People without animals had even stranger notions about them if they had any notions about them at all. It was as if animals were an invisible race, a population whose inner lives had gone undocumented and unnoticed for the whole of history, with few exceptions. That they lived lives of emotion, pleasure and great suffering, often as a direct result of our actions, didn't seem to interest or concern most people. But here they were, these feeling perhaps even thinking beings, living among us at our mercy as we used and abused them for entertainment, food and labor. It must have been easier that way, I thought, not to know what animals felt. The weight of their devotion, sorrow, fear and hatred would have been too much to bear.

Or to put it differently, pets are people too. It was another of my collectible slogans that got rejected. Whoever was in charge of the meeting that day probably didn't have a pet, or if he did he saw it as entertainment for his children, a kind of warm-blooded video game. But pet people would have understood. They would have bought a million of those.

It hadn't been my choice to live alone with a bunch of four-legged people, but now that I did I didn't want to hear what anyone had to say about it. I didn't want to talk about it or about anything else. I didn't want to talk, period. Not in person and not on the phone. Not at all, not ever, at least not in the foreseeable future. That was another thing I liked about my animals. They didn't talk, and didn't care if I did, though Bob occasionally tried, howling in a way reminiscent of Patty Duke's portrayal of Helen Keller in *The Miracle Worker* that sounded like he was trying to pronounce the word walk.

CHAPTER 12

P'i / Standstill (Stagnation)

In times of stagnation, attend to your attitude.

What you notice about animals when you're alone with them for extended periods of time is that, in addition to being variations on the theme that is their species, they have distinct personalities of their own, like humans except usually nicer. Gregoire for instance was self-absorbed and even selfish though so charming and beautiful we'd never minded. He wasn't stupid but he pretended to be, ignoring directions when they didn't suit him. Once, at the height of Phillip's and my happy home life, at a birthday party we threw for a friend, Gregoire, who'd been staying with us for weeks, bored a hole into the side of the cake, which had been set on a low table. Phillip had commissioned the cake from an artisan baker and it was fashioned in the shape of the honoree's architecturally significant house. Gregoire had poked his nose straight through a butter-cream skylight. He withdrew his snout when we shouted but as he did he opened his mouth, like a molly screw that enters the wall as a single prong and then butterflies open once it's inside.

It was an act of rebellion, an insouciant fuck-you moment I secretly admired. We yelled some more and he removed himself just far enough to watch the repair of the cake—I promised I'd eat the dog-sullied piece—but as soon as we finished and turned away he stuck his nose back in. You may say this was merely the act of a dumb, hungry beast, but I say it was the doing of a cagey and lawless charmer, one without malice but also without remorse.

Bob would never do such a thing. If Gregoire was indifferent to the wishes of others, Bob was the opposite, exquisitely sensitive, watching us with an expression of concern so deep it suggested his heart was breaking for us. Maybe he was some kind of saint, a Bodhisattva, at the very least a good citizen. Bobbysattva, I called him when no one was around, he who'd returned for one last incarnation to demonstrate the nature of selfless love. I'm afraid the lesson was lost on us.

Bob had a deeply knowing nature; even the skeptical and unsentimental had to acknowledge that. If spoken to harshly, he'd lie down with an elaborate show of sorrow and refuse to eat. When I was sad he grew still and licked my face. At moments like this he flattened his ears to make his head smooth and round with only his glamorous eyelashes sticking out. When guests were due to arrive he sat in front of the door like an expectant sphinx. When they left he mourned their departure. If I thought of taking him for a walk, he stood up; if I thought of napping, he trotted down the hall to stand beside the bed; and when I thought of throwing away his torn plastic bone, his face drooped into a harlequin mask of fright and he ran to hide it from me. Bob was a mensch, a comic, a psychic and a saint.

So when Gregoire had his inevitable seizure, two days after Diane dropped him off, I wasn't surprised that Bob stood guard in a wide-legged stance, his orange brows knitted together with concern. Afterward he licked Gregoire's face and lay down next to him in a watchful pose, refusing to budge until at last Greg struggled to his feet looking confused and wobbled to the back door to be let out to pee.

That evening, after Gregoire seemed to have recovered, I asked him, "What do you need?" and into my head, with complete clarity, came two words: "water" and "toast."

I brought him his water bowl and he lapped up a little messily but then looked at me with those unfocused, filmy little eyes and cocked his head wishfully as if to say thanks but where's the toast? So I went to the kitchen and dropped a slice of slightly stale rye bread into the toaster. When it popped up I buttered it, considered jam but decided against it, cut it into quarters and brought it to him on a blue china plate. He bent his head and ate, crunching methodically and wagging his bushy tail slightly in rhythm with his crunching. Then he slumped down right there on the kitchen floor and fell asleep, toast crumbs still clinging to his gray muzzle.

It was a small moment but to me it felt like the sign I'd been waiting for. I tried again. Every day I asked him and Bob simple questions and then waited for an answer and usually got one in the form of a single word or phrase that popped into my head. It required a kind of passive openness, a receptivity to the unknown. It was the pet communication version of Keats' negative capability but the thing it most reminded me of was what I was told was supposed to happen when you pray.

"If you keep talking! And asking for favors! God doesn't have a doggone chance in heck to get a word in edgewise!" I remembered Paul Peterson, the sweaty, red-faced youth minister, had shouted this one Sunday evening at a youth group service in the damp church basement lounge when I last attended church at the age of fourteen.

"You gotta say, Lord! Jesus! Tell me what to do! And then you gotta shut up and listen to the answer!" He shouted this admonition at us in a fake Southern accent. I knew for a fact he'd grown up in Naperville, in far southwest suburban Chicago, and gone to Wheaton Bible College less than thirty miles from his childhood home. But when he preached he did it in a North Carolina accent.

I liked the idea though. It took the pressure off me, kept me from always having to keep up my end of the conversation with God and be interesting and sincere and word my requests just right. I would have happily listened if God had seemed interested in talking but prayer hadn't ever worked for me—passive or active. This conversation with dogs seemed like a version of it that might, maybe because I wasn't asking for anything for myself.

I began to try it on the dogs at the pet store getting groomed. The trouble with that was not that it didn't work but that it did. I started to get replies. I heard complaints, demands, requests I had no way of fulfilling. Most asked for water or to make the combing stop and I sent vaguely reassuring messages saying they had to be patient, that soon it would stop and they could have a drink and go home. But other requests were more worrisome. I'm anxious, my eye hurts, I can't breathe right with all these chemical smells in the room, this person smells sick. I am sick. I am uncomfortable, I have to pee, I have to empty my bowels. I will die soon. Or worst of all, simply, I am afraid.

This shapeless fear I felt coming from the grooming room unsettled me, reminded me of someone or something naggingly familiar that I couldn't place. Then one day while watching a skittish Bichon Frise have burrs removed from her paw I remembered. The fearful dogs reminded me of my mother.

CHAPTER 13

T'ung Jên / Fellowship With Others

In fellowship with others,
embody the principles of the Sage.

My mother had my sister and me late, for those days, after her theatrical ambitions faltered and faded, not out of any desire for children but because it was time to settle down. She'd taken a job as a high school drama teacher, a job her father found for her and pushed her to accept but which she'd quit in the middle of winter term when some prankish boy with a crush picked the lock of her new Rambler and left an obscene valentine on the driver's seat. Weeks later, at a loss for what to do next, she said yes to dinner with my father, whose desk in the Humanities office had been next to hers and who'd had his eye on her since the day she'd agreed to coach one of his remedial English students in diction and showed up in a snug cocoa-colored sweater set and a flared plaid skirt, carrying a copy of *Othello*. Six months later they were married and she was pregnant.

Photographs of her from those days show a nervous-looking small-boned beauty, with wavy dark hair, milky skin and movie-star legs. She wore scarves, pedal pushers, sunglasses in these photos, sometimes all at once. By the time I knew her though she'd grown softer and differently beautiful. Something haunted had crept up around her eyes, a faraway look of patient disappointment. Her outfits alternated between immaculate and slovenly, depending on her mood. There's a photo of her taken when she must have been forty-two or -three standing next to Susan at some school event; Susan is holding a large trophy that partly obscures my mother's face. The photo shows how much she'd changed, easy to see next to her firstborn, who was a vibrant, undisappointed, thinner, younger version of herself. I appear with my mother and sister in some of these photos—my father was the cameraman—but even as a small child I seemed to be a foundling. Blonder, blander, bigger, bulkier, boringly reliable, I look embarrassed to know I'd grow up to be the one who handled the money when we went out to lunch.

I was my mother's favorite but I feared it was by default, not for any qualities I possessed but rather for those I lacked. A deal was struck early on that I would not be too pretty. I was her plain and undramatic sidekick, the one she could count on to never move away and never show her up—unlike Susan who'd left at eighteen and returned for exactly three days a year and never at holidays. My mother seemed both hurt and relieved she was gone—it was easier to admire Susan from a distance than it was to be in the same room with her—but my father pined for her the rest of his life. And if I'd once been fatuous enough to hope that the emptiness created by Susan's departure would advance me to her position of honor, I soon learned that love doesn't work that way.

I never really knew what my mother was thinking. She always seemed to be keeping a secret, seemed to live her real life slightly apart from the rest of us and behind the closed curtain of her pale gray eyes. It was hard to get her attention. She seemed to be in thrall to an inner world she never described but which appeared to contain many dangers. Balloons terrified her, as did certain seemingly harmless garbage collectors, a hearse she'd seen driving behind her once and the proximity of mayonnaise to her food. She was afraid of the dental hygienist, the shampoo girl though not the hairdresser, and sleep itself, that would-be knitter-up of the raveled sleeve of care, although she did plenty of it or tried to if only during the day when light made it safe. She was afraid of elevators, turbans and the sight of men with rakes, though I suspect some of the things she claimed to fear, like going to church and talking to the neighbors, she simply detested but was too polite to admit.

For a while as a child, instead of laughing at my mother's fears, as Susan did, I tried to deprogram her. I ate watermelon seeds by the tablespoonful to demonstrate they would not make me pregnant. I chatted conspicuously with the garbage man and lived to tell about it. She went along with these early psychological experiments, indulgently pretending to be helped by them but with an indifferent, world-weary air. She saw the ghost behind the veil. Over the years I gave up trying to help, seeing that her fears were not for me but for herself and that they had grown into something more than fear, into convictions, beliefs, and that she would not be talked out of them.

She got sick about a year after Phillip and I moved into the house—we were on vacation when my father placed the only international phone call of his life to reach us at the villa we were renting in Costa Rica to summon us home—but because hospitals were among the things she either feared or detested, she refused to go. So she lay in her bed at home weighed down not by flesh—she was eight-nine pounds by then—but by some terrible grief we could see in her but which she never named. She appeared to mourn things in her life that either had happened or that should have but did not, things of which she never spoke, at least to me, and which, in her younger days, had caused her to suffer excesses of anger followed by waves of regret and resulted in a lethargy that finally confined her to bed where she refused to eat or speak, a tiny woman with an iron will dying in a tantrum of resistance. The family doctor came and went. He tested her blood and her heart and when he found nothing wrong concluded, with shocking simplicity, that she didn't want to live.

To have this deeply-known but never acknowledged fact medically confirmed was deflating. We'd known it all along but we didn't want to be right, we wanted it to be something else, a namable disease that would make it not our fault. It's not about the body after all my father and Phillip and I agreed, shaking our heads after the doctor had left the little downstairs bedroom my father had set up for her, where he brought her trays of food she wouldn't touch. We saw clearly then how her life was not and never had been about her body, that her physical beauty, perhaps even her sexual life and motherhood had been events that had happened to her, but were not at all who she was. These things that had happened, including my sister and me, were energy-consuming, passing occurrences that interrupted her thoughts but ultimately didn't hold her attention. Once she decided it was time to stop living she began, almost gratefully, to die.

We felt dismissed, or at least my father and I did—Susan was in Minneapolis accepting an award. We felt offended to be so summarily departed from, my father especially, whose cooking efforts had been aimed at keeping my mother cheered up for decades. But we had no choice; she had decided it was time to go and we had to accept it.

I sat by her bed. She was afraid, I could tell, but she wouldn't talk about it, maybe partly out of bravery but mostly because she didn't trust any of us to understand. She just waited for it to be over. Once I suggested, pretending a shabby fake optimism I adopted in times of distress, that she try a game to calm herself, something I did to make myself fall asleep at night. Go through the alphabet, I suggested, my own fear bringing out my worst Pollyanna self, and name something soothing for each letter. A for angels for instance, I said idiotically, still fresh off a day of composing smarmy angel poems. B for baths, C for cauliflower, D for dogs.

I couldn't get the tone right. I was trying to talk her out of fear she had every right to and she was not only not comforted, she was annoyed, searching for my face in the murkiness that was all that was left of her fading vision. She didn't need eyes, though, to see my cheerfulness was fake, to see she had given birth to a fool. She was the one who was dying but she felt sorry for me. Finally she patted my hand and spoke what may have been her last words to me, "You know, dear, that I'm afraid of angels." It was a reprimand. Gentle but still, I should have known.

"I just want to help," I said.

"I know," she said, closing her eyes. Her voice was whispery but her diction, as always, was perfect.

So to listen to lives vibrating with pride and fear was familiar. And though I knew my mother would consider it a shabby tribute that the nervous, tear-stained Bichon Frise on the Petsmart grooming table reminded me of her, it was the best I could do. I hadn't been able to help her much but I wondered if I could do better this time, or at least do a better job of trying.

CHAPTER 14

Ta Yü / Possession in Great Measure

*Those who are steadfastly balanced, humble, and in
harmony with the Sage inherit everything under the sun.*

My friend Donna had been trying to get me to join her as a volunteer dog walker at Angels, the animal shelter where she worked,
where I'd adopted Bob and she'd gotten her viszla mix Vladimir
Putin. She said his smooth head and pink eyes reminded her of
the Russian president and she intended to call him Vladdy but
took to calling him Putey Poot instead when George Bush conferred the nickname and in reference to the dog's chronic flatulence. I called him Vlad, a dog, in honor of my favorite book in
fourth grade.

Bob and I and Vlad and Donna regularly met at the park in
the mornings since she was my only dog-walking friend who knew
I'd quit my job and because she was willing to go early sometimes. Lately she had increased her efforts to get me to come to
the shelter with her. For years I had made up excuses for why I
couldn't do it, donating money instead, back when I had a job, and
even writing a rhyming slogan for the shelter which they printed
on T-shirts and sold at their fundraisers: *Puppies are angels
in furry disguise, you can tell by the love you see in their eyes.*
There was a version for cats too.

But now that I had more time and less money I couldn't think
of a good excuse not to go except for the truth, which was too
cowardly to utter. It made me sad. I wanted to help but I didn't
want to be around all that neediness. I knew it was a lame excuse
so, when, about a week after the toast incident with Gregoire, she
brought it up again, I surprised us both by saying yes.

The smell of shit, piss and fear mixed with Lysol met us long before we saw a single dog and that, on top of the cacophonous barking, reminded me of how much I hadn't wanted to come.

Donna was more practical, never letting aesthetics slow her down for good or ill. "This way," she said, striding ahead of me in her extra large overalls and hiking boots through an antiseptic waiting room straight into a hallway that passed between two aisles of dog runs, cages that opened out back onto little plots of dirt where the more fastidious dogs performed their excretions. Attached to the front of each cage was a clipboard on which the dog's name and history were posted along with a record of the attentions paid to it that week.

Caesar, Champ, Emma, Dudley. Each dog had once been named, if only when it arrived at the shelter. The names suggested a moment of attention paid to the nuances of its personality or its unique physical being, each representing some spark of affection at least strong enough to inspire this single act of naming. Amelia, Fluffernut, Bosco, Priscilla. Noah, Demeter, Samantha, Thor.

Some dogs lunged at us, howling and flinging themselves at the bars of their cages as we passed; others slumped deject-edly in their corners, stinking of shit. The last time I'd been here was to pick out Bob, who was then named Mike Tyson. Phillip had reluctantly agreed to a shelter dog, planning instead to buy an English setter puppy from a breeder in Wales. When the deal fell through—we got a call at our hotel in Betws-y-Coed saying the puppy had died—he'd agreed to just look when we got home. Handsome and civilized, neither fierce nor timid, Bob had observed us both through the bars of his cage with such self-confi-dent charm and evident robust health that even Phillip found him irresistible. We named him Roberto after that same right fielder we later named Clement for, but I called him Bob.

Now I was back, nauseated by the smells and guilty I wasn't even going to take one dog home this time. Donna led me into the backyard where another volunteer was playing with a pit bull mix and some kind of hound. We were her relief. She pointed to two more dogs in a holding pen. Donna and I were each given a blue nylon leash and off we went, following a well-worn path around the empty lot in back. Donna got Sheba, a gentle emaciated greyhound, while I got a panting old black shepherd mix with a huge lump on his side and a limp. A limp and a lump. He was Toro, a name I hoped had been inspired by the long-gone vigor and admirable stubbornness of his youth.

"What kind of asshole would give up an old dog?" Donna was often furious on behalf of animals. I admired her passion but I was just sad and feeling worse by the minute.

"Maybe there were extenuating circumstances," I said hopefully, trying to fend off the buzzy feelings I was getting from the dogs that I couldn't process because I was trying to talk to Donna. The young greyhound was keeping a good pace and Toro was lagging behind so I said, "You go ahead, we're going to take it easy." After we slowed down I started to listen.

Immediately the dog stopped walking. And looked me in the eyes. Now for people who know dogs, and cats, you know that when they look at you they mean something. Sometimes it's a request or even a command in the case of cats, but sometimes it's just an existential greeting, the kind people passing in an airport telegraph to each other: *Hello, I know you're in there but let's agree not to discuss it*. That's what this look was. Toro settled his stiff body down on the dirt in the path and continued to stare amiably at me, still panting. The sun beat down on his dark back. I sat cross-legged in the brown grass next to him and stared back, going into my prayerful open mind mode, and waited.

Maybe I heard something and maybe I didn't, and I can't quote exactly what I thought I heard because dogs don't use language the way we do. They send messages in the form of pictures or feelings, which, as far as I can tell, our brains translate back into the only language we feel certain of, words. It's imperfect, like reading a Chinese poem in English that was first translated into French. You just have to trust the translator not to take too much poetic license.

What I heard Toro say was something like this: "This is good, hot sun, nice. Please scratch my ear. Very good. I am tired. I miss my friend. Your scent reminds me of someone I once knew when I was young. Dear. A little drink would be nice. I am so tired. Shall we go back now? I'd like that if you don't mind. Thank you. I like you."

It was something like that although words cannot fully describe it, how emotionally rich and resonant it was, nuanced, like when you awaken from a dream with a feeling that is far deeper and more poignant than the ridiculous events that inspired that feeling. Toro's message was tender, soulful. There were subtle hints of yearning, compassion even—for whom, though? Me? Also resignation and a little regret though not so much as I expected. And nothing about the big lump or the bad leg. Constant milk-chocolaty eye contact throughout this exchange. Then he heaved himself up, dragging the bad leg, and, with a glance over his shoulder at me as if to say, "You ready?" he led us back in his hobbling gait. He headed straight for his cage, accepting a last ear scratch and licking my hand before he went in to lie down.

Donna and I each walked four more dogs before we left that afternoon. When I got home I ran a bath and poured a glass of wine, drinking it in the tub while ignoring the ringing phone. When it rang again while I was dishing out trout feast to Clement I picked it up. It was Donna on the line; she was agitated.

"You can't believe what happened," she said. "I just got a call from the veterinarian at the shelter and he said that old dog you were walking, Toro? He died tonight. In his sleep. He wants you to call him back. His name's Dr. Barney."

I finished my wine and then I called the number. It was kind of a coincidence but Toro was old and how could Dr. Barney know what had happened. And what was the point of talking about it? Old dogs die. I hoped he didn't think it was my fault.

As I listened to the phone ring I refilled my glass and raised it in a toast to Toro. The animals seemed to understand. Clement, finished with his trout feast dinner, hopped up on my lap and began to knead my belly. Bob looked over his shoulder at me from where he was licking out Clement's bowl and locked eyes with me gravely. Gregoire trotted to my side, his toenails clicking on the kitchen floor, and breathed his smelly breath on me. The phone rang seven times before a gruff voice answered. "'Lo."

"May I speak with Dr. Barney? This is Maryanne Draper, the volunteer? Donna Kaminski asked me to call?"

"Oh, it's you. Wait a minute." There was a commotion on the other end of the line and then he came back sounding clearer. "Sorry, I was feeding the dogs. I mean my dogs. Listen I don't want to bother you but I called Donna because I found Toro dead tonight when I made my final bed check before leaving. I was just wondering if you'd noticed anything unusual. I keep track and I didn't see this one coming quite so soon."

I didn't know what to say. It wasn't a surprise to me. I hoped he didn't hold me responsible but as far as I could tell Toro was getting ready to die and was waiting until he could say goodbye to someone. I wasn't sure I could say this to this Dr. Barney person over the phone though. On the other hand, why not. I topped off my wine. Ever since I'd quit my job I cared less and less about other people's opinions.

"Well, doctor, to tell you the truth . . ."

"Stan, please. Call me Stan."

"OK. Stan. Since you asked." I ended up telling him the whole story. I told him about Gregoire and the toast incident and the messages from the dogs on the grooming table.

"Hmmm," he said noncommittally. "Is that it? About Toro I mean? No vomiting or seizures or anything? Just this vibe thing, is that right?"

"Yeah. He was panting a lot but otherwise he seemed OK, pretty happy even."

"OK, well, thanks for calling." Just before he hung up I could hear deep-throated barking in the background.

Chapter 15

Ch'ien / Modesty

*The Creative acts to empty what is full and
to offer abundance to what is modest.*

The next day I had to finish a product outline for a series of Princess Di reproduction earrings and write a poem for each one. The first pair was based on earrings Diana appeared to wear in a shadowy photograph from a White House dinner. Each subsequent pair in the series of twelve would coincide with an important event and would contain a different birthstone crystal, one for each month. The trick was to figure out a way to make people buy the whole set rather than just their own birthstones. My idea was to link the birthstones to astrological signs. I sat at my computer reciting the rhymes I'd written that would be engraved into each earring box.

I'd started with Aries. *Aries is feisty and stubborn and smart. She knows who she is and she did from the start.* It sounded good but it didn't really say much and there were eleven more to go. I kept a kitchen timer on my desk for this kind of writing. I decided to give myself five minutes per poem and then move on to the next sign. That was exactly an hour to make it through the entire horoscope on the first draft. The trick was to not spend hours rewriting them the next day.

I was on Virgo (*the virgin seems pure and serene and demure but under the calm you can hear that girl purr*) wondering if it seemed a little risqué for the intended demographic when the phone rang. I hesitated, staring at the screen. Maybe slightly bawdy was good, maybe they should all be a little wanton. (*Libra wants sex and not just a little; she's sick of that guy who's so noncommittal.*) Just slightly provocative might work, I thought. Women that age, who buy this stuff, my age actually, wanted. . . . The phone rang again. I picked up the receiver, figuring it would be my old boss calling to ask if I had the rhymes ready yet.

"Stan here."

"Stan. Oh. Stan. I thought it was someone else."

"Sorry. I was wondering. Um. Donna said you were out of work?"

"She did? Well, that's not exactly true. Not really. I mean I quit my job. But to freelance. In fact I'm working on something right now. I write these poems? I mean like rhymes, to go on products. Freelance." I was talking too much but there was no good way to explain it.

"Yeah, well then I won't take too much time. I called to ask if you'd consider coming in here sometimes. To do what we were talking about last night. Just sometimes, I mean not as a volunteer but as a job, part time. I'd pay you."

"You'd pay me."

"Yeah. To kind of you know sound out the dogs or whatever, talk to them about their health and well-being. As an experiment. I couldn't pay you much. But I'd pay you."

"Really? Well. Sure. I'm working on something now. But I could come tomorrow."

"That would be good," he said and then, "Tell me again what is it you do?"

"I'm a freelance writer? I mean I used to have this job but I quit and just kept the writing part and now I do it freelance." I knew I sounded apologetic and I listened for a response, permission to stop, but when I heard nothing I continued. "It's kind of hard to describe. I write these sayings to go on products? You wouldn't think there was a need for that but actually there is. Like now I'm writing these astrological poems to go with birthstone jewelry. I mean they're not really poems in the true sense. More like doggerel, jingles?"

Finally Stan said "ah." Like maybe he had his finger up a cat's ass and wasn't really listening.

"Like what sign are you? I mean, as an example."

"You mean me? Oh—I think Taurus."

"See, here's what I wrote about you: Taurus is sexy, silent and cute. He loves music and food and the Art Institute. The meter's a little off—I'm not done yet—but you get the idea. I know, it sounds childish. They're really fixated on rhyme there."

I waited. Nothing. I blushed. I had to get off the phone.

Instead I said, "Does that sound like you at all though?"

"Well. Sort of I guess. I like the Art Institute. So when do you want to start? Tomorrow I mean."

"Nine o'clock?"

"OK. Just come to the front desk and have me paged."

CHAPTER 16

Yü / Enthusiasm

Proper enthusiasm opens every door.

I figured I should wear jeans. Donna said she wore overalls because the dogs jump but then she always wore overalls including when she saw her patients at the eating disorder clinic where she is a part-time psychotherapist. But overalls seemed like an overtly non-sexual message that I wasn't quite ready to send. It seemed like giving up. Not that I had any designs on Stan who in fact I had never met though he did have a nice voice. Jeans and a long-sleeved black T-shirt, I thought, to protect my arms and so the mud wouldn't show. Sneakers for traction.

When I got there the place was already buzzing with activity. An earnest looking middle-aged couple sat in orange plastic bucket chairs filling out an adoption form; somebody was carrying around a traumatized looking cat that had been left outside over-night in a too-small carrier.

Stan showed up wearing a dingy white doctor's smock over jeans. He was short and burly and had wavy gray hair with what looked like pieces of blue chenille blanket stuck in it and tortoise shell glasses that magnified his green eyes. He led me to an examining room.

"Here's what I'm thinking," he said after shaking my hand and settling me on a stool under a fluorescent light with a Styrofoam cup of lukewarm instant coffee. When he handed me the coffee I caught a whiff of him. He smelled like sawdust. "Could you come one day a week and kind of make the rounds with me and tell me what you're hearing? We could try it for a month and see. I'm interested to see if what you're picking up sheds any light on the dogs' medical conditions or the circumstances of their coming here."

"OK," I said, "but could we bring them in one at a time? It might be easier for me to focus. And I don't know how many I could do in a day. It might be better to break it up—it's actually pretty intense. Maybe half a day twice a week?"

We worked out a deal. He wasn't kidding about the money; he couldn't pay much but it was OK, more than I'd be making waiting for someone to call with another freelance job. At least, I thought, I'd be doing something constructive.

We agreed to start right away. The first patient was a three-legged, nine-year-old Yorkie named Cleo. She clearly had an itching problem, for which she was being treated. This I or anyone could see. I heard her tell me she was thirsty. Stan filled up a water bowl and she drank. Like the arthritic Toro, she didn't complain about her leg situation at all.

Then we saw a cattle dog, a lab mix and a caramel colored pit bull named Louise with fighting scars on her back. All were thirsty. None had anything else to say, as far as I could tell, except for Louise who wanted to know about Bob's smell on my shoes and sleeves. I felt like I was on the spot and I thought about making something up. It would be easy to say the pit bull told me she felt she wanted more affection after a life of exploitation. She probably didn't receive many gratuitous pats from passersby, but I didn't hear that. She seemed to feel fine except for thirst. I figured I wasn't being paid enough to worry about earning my keep and decided to play it safe by telling the truth.

We went through the whole morning like this without much happening other than learning that nobody got enough fresh water.

By twelve thirty Stan said he was going to break for lunch and did I want to join him before I took off. We went to Subway where he ordered a meatball sandwich and a bag of Fritos. I had a cheese and veggie sub on wheat bread. I apologized for not coming up with anything.

"That's OK," he said, "let's just keep trying for awhile. You'll come back tomorrow and we'll see how it goes." He wiped ketchup from his mustache.

The next morning I arrived again at nine o'clock. Stan was already at the front desk, signing in pet food and paper towel donations because the intake lady had called in sick.

He led me to his examining room. Bonnie, his nurse, brought in a shaggy mixed breed, maybe shepherd and chow, then a golden retriever, then a lab mix. It was like the day before but with the fluorescent light turned off as I'd requested, I felt more in tune with the animals. Still, no one had much to say, other than social niceties. I like you, who is that dog I smell on your clothes? Do you have anything for me to eat? I am thirsty.

The next dog was a lanky skittery soft black lab named Harvey, about a year old, a little manic and very friendly. He was skinny enough that Stan easily hoisted him onto the examining table. I sat politely opposite and looked him in the eye, asking permission to pet him. He smiled, as dogs do, slid around the table on his toenails and said he was thirsty. He said I was nice. He began to sniff me.

He lodged his nose in my armpit and bumped it against my right breast. Sniffed. Sniffed again. I began to feel nervous. He looked me in the eye and said, "Not normal but no problem. I want to go home with you. I'm lonely."

I reported this to Stan though I didn't tell him I had breast fibroids and that I was relieved that Harvey had paused to notice and then seemed to dismiss them as the benign tumors I'd been told they were. Subtle dog, I thought, despite his goofy demeanor. Stan didn't say anything but made some notes and after we saw a few more dogs, including one that distinctly said that something was wrong with her ear, we agreed to call it a day and that I would come back next week on the same schedule.

"So what about Harvey?" I said.

"What about him. Do you want another animal?"

"Not really but it was such a direct request I feel bad ignoring it."

"He just got here, he's a puppy. He'll get used to it."

We avoided eye contact. Then he said, "We do foster them out though. We post their pictures online as puppies-in-training and then place them in foster homes to socialize them. When they're ready we adopt them out. The idea is if someone can teach them to sit and walk on a leash and calm down a little they'll be more adoptable and there's less likelihood they'll be returned a month later.

"Hmmm," I said.

"We'd give you a stipend for food. You're probably too busy though."

"You're quite a salesman," I said.

CHAPTER 17

Sui / Following

Do not argue with what is.
Simply follow the progress of truth.

After several failed attempts to get him to sit down and stay in the back, Harvey settled into the front seat of my thirteen-year-old Volkswagen alongside a large bag of puppy food. Occasionally he leaned across the gearshift to rest his head in my lap, leaving a damp spot composed of spit and leftover vomit. He was a little whiskery around the mouth and bits of vomit clung to his beard. He'd only thrown up once, producing a neat puddle on the floor, a slightly bubbly mixture of what appeared to be newsprint, hair and undigested kibble. He looked wild-eyed as he slid across the torn seat at sudden stops but otherwise seemed happy. Even when he tried to climb into my lap it seemed more out of companionability than fear and he good-naturedly accepted it when I elbowed him off. The next car should be an automatic, I thought; dogs and gearshifts don't mix.

I stopped at Donna's on the way home. Stan had given me a stack of flyers she had promised to pin up around town advertising the annual pet shelter fair. Donna wasn't there. She and Vlad were off on a round of pet therapy visits, but I had a key so I let myself in and set the flyers on the kitchen table. An embroidered yellow pillow commanded "Smile! God loves you!" from an uncomfortable kitchen chair. It replaced the one Felicia had insisted on keeping there with the Dorothy Parker quote on it. I had always liked Felicia and I preferred "What fresh hell is this?" but when she dumped Donna for a racket ball-playing stockbroker, the pillow disappeared.

I hated being there when Donna wasn't. The place was terrifyingly clean and I was afraid I'd leave some shaming sign of my presence. I hated even walking on her gleaming floors. Donna lived alone now, except for Vlad, on the ground floor of the red brick two-flat she and Felicia had bought together in the salad days of their relationship. Felicia was a monumental slob and when she'd moved out Donna had purged the place of her, cleaning every inch with righteous anger and never letting it get dirty again. Vlad was the cleanest dog I knew. I backed out the door feeling demoralized at the thought of returning to my messy house, which was about to become messier with the addition of a third dog.

I brought Harvey in through the front door on his nylon shelter leash, figuring that since this is where guests entered, back when Phillip and I used to have guests, Bob could think of him as a guest. Bob liked guests.

Bob and Gregoire rushed the door, Bob bouncing on his stiff back legs, crouching to sniff Harvey front and back and making a little guttural exhalation when Harvey tried to sniff him back. Gregoire barked in his high-pitched voice and ran circles around them both. Bob's little growl was enough to make Harvey flop submissively onto the floor but when he turned to walk away Harvey jumped up and tried to follow him into the kitchen.

An agreement about status had been reached. I unsnapped Harvey's leash and they were off, up and down the hall, Harvey careening into walls and Bob showing him the ropes, herding and policing him and trying to avoid Gregoire's irrelevant attempts to herd them both. Clement sat rolled up in an orange ball observing all this from his perch on the kitchen table and when Harvey got too close he turned his back and floated away.

They were all going to get along fine. My animals were the most socially well-adjusted beings I knew.

CHAPTER 18

Ku / Work on What Has Been Spoiled (Decay)

A challenge to improvement: that which has been spoiled through neglect can be rejuvenated through effort.

We, Bob and I with Gregoire as an audience, spent the next two days introducing Harvey to all the dog routines I normally fit into a week. We walked to the park morning and night, all three dogs on a separate leash, my arms pulling out of their sockets and scissoring in front of me as the dogs rushed from scent to scent. We drove to the big dog park in the afternoon. The first night Donna came over with two bottles of red wine and we drank them both while I made pasta—see below—and my dogs played with Vlad in the backyard. I put Bob through his paces of sit and down and come to show Harvey how it worked and he caught on right away while Gregoire stood by and watched with his head cocked, feeling left out because he'd never learned to follow directions. Harvey followed Bob everywhere, mimicking all his moves, and when he didn't Bob acted the enforcer, grabbing the extra skin on his neck and tugging, especially on bathroom drills. But Harvey never had an accident and in three days he'd learned the routine.

Sleeping was a little trickier but they even worked that out without much intervention from me. Now that Phillip was gone Bob considered the bed his territory. He'd made a concession for Clement through some mysterious negotiation so that if Clement wasn't out hunting, he was free to come and go in the bed as he pleased. But Clement had seniority and he was small. As the newcomer and the youngest, though nearly as big as Bob, Harvey was the animal with least status so on the first night when he tried to follow us into bed, Bob ordered him out with his rare but authoritative growl and Harvey exited without protest or any apparent shame to Bob's bed on the floor. Meanwhile restless Gregoire jumped in and out of the bed a few times and then removed himself to sleep on the couch. Finally we were all settled. As I went to sleep that first night with all the animals in their places I felt satisfied and surrounded by friends. I said goodnight to each by name out loud.

Dog Party Pasta
Vegetarian version for Donna

Sauté in olive oil:
> Two cloves minced garlic
> One chopped red onion
> Lots of chopped parsley or cilantro.
> More herbs—oregano etc.

Boil a pound of penne.

Mix the vegetables and herbs with the pasta and grate in half a pound of pecorino cheese. If you don't have pecorino, use parmesan.

For meat eaters, add a pound of crumbled hot Italian sausage.

Chapter 19

Lin / Approach

Good approaches the superior person.

Stan called Saturday morning from the clinic to see how it was going with Harvey.

"OK," I said. "A second dog is a lot easier than the first. Or I guess I should say a third is easier than a second. Bob is training Harvey and Gregoire isn't too jealous. Sometimes they nap in a pile. There's a lot of hair though."

"Yeah, I was hoping it would work that way," he said. "They usually train each other. See you next week, same schedule?"

"OK," I said, cracking an egg into a bowl full of ground meat and tossing the shell to the dogs.

"Whatcha making?" Stan said.

"Meatloaf. Gregoire, cut it out. Get down from there."

"I'll see you next week," Stan said and hung up as I whisked the mixing bowl out from under Gregoire's open—was he drooling?—mouth. He cocked his head affably, still standing with both paws on the counter like a man about to eat lunch at a stand-up diner. I could tell he was wondering why the food had suddenly disappeared.

I was making meatloaf a day early for my father's usual four o'clock Sunday dinner visit because it tasted better the second day. He ate less and less these days but I made the same amount I always had and sent the leftovers home with him, keeping him in groceries for days.

This Sunday I was serving one of his favorite meals—meatloaf, mashed potatoes and cauliflower, cooked very soft, with cheddar cheese sauce. Apple pie and ice cream for dessert.

Had Stan been angling for a dinner invitation? I wondered as I stirred the eggs into the meat.

Sunday Meatloaf

Mix together a pound of ground beef and a pound of ground pork.

Mix in 2 large eggs. I always use free-range chicken eggs, though they're twice as expensive as the regular kind, because I want to believe that the birds that lay them lead easier lives. You could say I am conflicted about animal products in food though most of what I eat requires the servitude if not outright death of a being with a brain and I appreciate how unappetizing it is to say so within the context of a recipe. But now that I've begun I must say that eggs are hardly the main issue. Notice I didn't even mention the real gaping guilty point in the first ingredient line, which calls for beef and pork, clever euphemistic French-derived words once meant to stand in for the coarser Anglo-Saxon names for the animals from whose bodies these meats come, the cow and the pig. My weak argument to justify my own meat-eating is that if animals can live happily their deaths aren't so unfair. I don't know if this is good enough in face of the fact that we breed creatures, create lives, only to kill and eat them. Or rather I suspect that it's not but it's better than nothing and all I can manage right now.

The shameful fact is I crave meat. I used to gorge on it and then vomit afterward feeling not only guilt but also sorrow as I flushed away the half-digested animal remains. Get over it, Phillip had said, annoyed, poking the pink steaks on the grill with a long fork while I wrung my hands. It's nature's order, he'd said. The large eat the small, the strong eat the weak, the smart eat the dumb and the tasty. It's just how it is. Look at Bob and Clement.

Donna and I agree not to discuss it though sometimes I hear her gasp when she opens my refrigerator. I thought I would become a vegetarian when Phillip left but somehow it didn't happen. The old foods are comforting and I haven't gotten around to it. And besides, I tell myself, my father needs protein.

Add Worcestershire sauce, salt and pepper.

Add breadcrumbs, about a cup. For years I made my own from stale bread, a nice thrifty thing to do, but they were always too coarse. Finally I gave in and bought a can of ready-made and I recommend it unless you have the patience and self-discipline to grind your own very fine. I never did. The canned ones are cheap, already seasoned and work much better.

Add chopped onions.

Add chopped parsley.

Add chopped carrots.

Add a small can of tomato paste. Or is it tomato sauce? I never remember but frankly it doesn't matter; either one works.

Mix it all up and cook it in the oven at 350 degrees for about an hour in a bread pan. Keep an extra bread pan around just for meatloaf.

It's done when it forms a crust and shrinks away from the edges of the pan. It keeps well and tastes better the second day.

CHAPTER 20

Kuan / Contemplation

By concentrating on the higher laws
you acquire the power that underlies them.

My father was slower this Sunday, as he had been every Sunday for months. Three months? Four? How long was it since I'd begun to notice a decline? It took him longer than ever from when his car arrived at the curb—announced by Bob and Gregoire and now by Harvey in imitation of them both in loud excited barking—to unfold himself out of the driver's seat and make his way to my front door. He did not want to be helped. He hobbled up the long driveway, clutching a plastic bag full of mushrooms he'd stopped to collect on the side of the highway on the drive over and leaning on his ancient cane, one that had belonged to his own father and which he would not replace with the uglier but sturdier three-pronged aluminum version I'd bought him. Usually I let Bob run out to greet him. Bob knew better than to knock him down, was positively decorous with him though he could have flattened him in a second. He and Greg would have been too much though, and Harvey made it impossible. They were all barking now and wild to go out and meet him but I leashed Harvey and grabbed Greg by his big ruff and opened the door when my father finally reached it.

"You get another mutt?" he said, poking Harvey's ribs with the rubber tip of his cane and reaching out to pat Bob and Gregoire who were squirming like huge hairy smiling eels around his skinny legs. Harvey was straining at the leash to get at my father too, panting and choking as I held him tight.

"No, this is Harvey, Dad," I shouted over the din. "He's the foster dog, from the shelter? Where I work? Remember I told you? I'll just train him and give him back."

Now that I had to explain it, like everything else in my life, it sounded kind of weird.

"Too much trouble," he said, lowering himself into a kitchen chair and making a face, something between a grimace and an ironic smirk. "You get paid for this?"

"Sure," I said. Something about my father made a liar of me.

"Here," he said, handing me the mushrooms. "Picked 'em myself. Good stuff. Put 'em in scrambled eggs, with chives."

After my father had settled down at the kitchen table with a plate of deviled eggs, a block of Swiss cheese, a dish of saltine crackers and a martini, I let Harvey off his leash. He ran in circles a few times and then sat down next to Bob who had positioned himself in his usual place of honor next to my father. As he sipped his martini both dogs stared at his food with mesmeric focus, drooling a little on the kitchen floor. Greg lay on his side in the middle of the room gazing into space and twitching his ears.

I threw bones and saltines into the yard and when the dogs ran after them I shut the door. We ate at the kitchen table. My father told me about his neighbors Becky and Havel who owned a restaurant and left homemade cabbage rolls on his back porch sometimes. After dinner we let the dogs back in and settled in front of the TV in the living room to watch Animal Planet, my father in his customary spot on the couch with Clement behind him looking over his shoulder and Bob stretched out next to him. Greg lay at his feet and Harvey trotted around looking for a spot to settle, eventually seating himself in front of my father's lap where he began to sniff his crotch.

"Hey get out of there you rascally bastard," my father said, poking him in the ribs with his cane. Harvey desisted only for a moment and then stuck his nose back between my father's legs. As I dragged Harvey away to the kitchen to distract him with a Milkbone he looked me in the eye and telegraphed "sick smell."

"What?" I said out loud. I spread soft cheese on the treat to keep his attention and to make the alternative to smelling my father's crotch especially rewarding.

"Sick," he said again, blandly, and then sat neatly to accept the treat, crunching loudly on the cheese-coated Milkbone. "How sick?" I asked but already I could sense the thought passing out of his head like a slide in a projector being changed and replaced by the next one, labeled "expectation of more cheese." Discussion closed.

After an hour of *The Planet's Funniest Videos* I packed up the leftovers in wax paper and Tupperware and carried them to my father's car in a shopping bag while he made his way slowly out the front door and down the path to the driveway. I'd added other food to the bag in addition to the leftovers and set all the groceries on the floor of the back seat. At 119 pounds my father weighed less than I did and needed all the calories I could send home with him. And it was getting difficult for him to shop. This, along with Becky's cabbage rolls, could hold him for a week. Here is what I gave him:

All the leftover deviled eggs
¾ meatloaf
All the leftover mashed potatoes
½ cauliflower with cheddar cheese sauce
Most of the apple pie
2 tangerines that had been sitting on the windowsill for a week and needed a good home
An open bag of potato chips I'd bought on a whim and already eaten too many of and would eat for breakfast the next morning unless I passed them on to him
3 bananas
2 cans of Coke

CHAPTER 21

Shih Ho / Biting Through

There is an obstacle to the expression of truth.
Withdrawal into quietness allows the Sage to moderate.

The next morning I threw the *I Ching* and got hexagram #17: Sui/Following. *Don't argue with what is; simply follow the progress of the truth.* In the text it said to continue to wait and rest. After I took the dogs for a walk I went back to bed in my dog-walking clothes and tried to take a nap. That wasn't what it meant, though, I knew, and, anyway, I couldn't sleep. I was avoiding rather than following the progress of truth.

I got back out of bed and wrote some more poems. I was working on astrological angels now. I was anxious and it felt good to work. *Aquarius, marry us, bury us, scary us, nefarious. Aquarius will carry us, through good times and hard.* I worked all day, took the dogs for three long walks, did the laundry, balanced my checkbook and went to bed feeling virtuous for a change.

The next day I was due back at the clinic at nine o'clock but I woke up early and was in the parking lot by eight-forty. Stan's Subaru was already there. We spent three hours meeting with dogs and learned that a Chihuahua recently had puppies in someone's garage and that a boxer mix had a bowel blockage.

"Good day," said Stan when we were done. "Next time you can be on your own. Just take notes and let me know what you find out."

"You really think this is doing any good?"

"Yeah I kind of think it is. Want some lunch?"

We went back to Subway. Stan ordered the same sandwich, meatballs with extra sauce. I order a veggie sub.

"So how's it working out with Harvey?" he asked when we got our sandwiches.

I told him about the visit with my father. "The thing is," I said, "he said the word twice. Sick."

"Tell your father to go get a check-up."

"What, because my dog said so? It's not that easy with him. He's a hard guy to tell anything to. And he hates doctors, no offense. Plus it wasn't even my dog, it was Harvey."

"So tell him Bob said it."

"Very funny."

When I got home I walked the dogs, made tea and thought about what Stan had said. Then I called my father. It was four in the afternoon and he was already cooking the next day's breakfast. He liked to make it the day before so it would soften in the pan overnight and he could look forward to eating it in the morning when he went to bed.

We discussed the breakfast project. Usually these days he made oatmeal or grits with leftover bits of other food mixed in: spinach, cheese, hot dogs, whatever he had around from his own cooking or my contributions or the neighbors'. He had a pot of grits on the stove now. He'd put in the leftover meatloaf and some of the scavenged mushrooms from Harms Woods and planned to add part of a lasagna the neighbor down the alley had brought him earlier in the day. After we talked about food for a while I broached the subject of his health.

"Dad, have you been to see a doctor lately? About your problem?"

"What problem?" he said. "Did I say I had a problem?"

"The one you were talking about Sunday. Remember?" He'd said he had trouble urinating. He'd also been complaining about how tired he was.

"Speak up!" he shouted.

"I was asking if you've been to see a doctor!" I shouted. "About being so tired?"

"I don't complain! Was I complaining? I hate complainers," he shouted into the phone.

"No, of course not," I shouted back. "I just mean I'm concerned because you said you had less energy and felt some pain! Maybe you should see a doctor!" It was hard to be subtle and persuasive when you had to shout. It made for a fighting atmosphere.

"I hate those goddamned bastards," he shouted even louder. "I made an appointment but let's not talk about it."

"When?" I shouted.

"I said I didn't want to talk about it!"

"Can I drive you?"

"No!"

"Will you tell me when you go?"

"Maybe," he said. "Maybe not. Now just shut up about it."

We left it at that. He'd never been polite and his grits were boiling.

CHAPTER 22

Pi / Grace

Inside, the strength of simplicity and self-knowledge.
Outside, the beauty of acceptance and gentleness.

"I need to hire an assistant," Stan said. He unwrapped his meatball sandwich with surgical precision. Almost two weeks had passed since Harvey's incident with my father and we were having our usual lunch after our morning session with the dogs. I'd spent a lot of time with a sheltie mix named Alfie, who had some kind of skin disease that made her hair fall out. They kept her dressed in snug children's T-shirts to keep her from gnawing at the raw wound; the shirts fit over her stout body like colorful sausage casings. This morning she'd been wearing a Spiderman shirt and complained that it made her feel foolish.

"Do you want the job? You could work flexible hours and include the dog whispering as part of it, just fit it in as you like. You know how to handle the animals. I could teach you the rest."

"I don't have a degree, like, in biology or psychology or anything remotely pertinent."

"Yeah I figured. Doesn't matter. Higher education doesn't seem to impress animals much. You'll pick it up. What is your degree in?"

"Two, actually," I said, embarrassed, keeping my eyes on the potato chip I was dragging out of its foil bag. "Nothing useful I'm afraid. Philosophy."

Stan made a kind of chuffing noise through his food. Now he was eating the rest of my veggie sub, which he had slathered with ketchup and mustard, squeezing little plastic packets of the condiments empty each time he took a bite.

"Oh that is useful."

"At least I had the sense to drop out before I finished my PhD."

"Too bad. We could be Drs. Draper and Barney. You're hired if you want it. PhD or no. I just can't. . . ."

"Yeah I know you can't pay much. It's OK."

"So how 'bout it?"

I told him I'd think it over.

Stan's offer reminded me of how little I'd been doing lately. Unless you counted what Betty, my therapist, used to call internal work. I'd been in therapy for four years, years before. It had seemed terribly important at the time although now I couldn't remember much about it except that afterward I felt well enough to move in with Phillip. The best advice Betty ever gave me, not including the time she told me a little lipstick wouldn't hurt, was to do one good thing for myself every day. She called it home-work. I was supposed to keep a list of these good deeds on an index card, which I kept in my purse. Once a week I brought the index card to her office and read the list out loud, like the home-work it was, sometimes embellishing slightly if the acts seemed too small. I'd carried the habit into my post-therapy life or tried to though sometimes all it amounted to was eating dinner from a plate instead of a pan until one day an index card fell out of my purse during one of my rare visits from Susan and she made me explain what it was.

"Jesus, Maryanne. ONE good thing a day?" she'd said, "You're pathetic. Try one hundred." It had never occurred to me to up the number.

Betty was a big proponent of internal work when something made you feel bad. She said it was OK to withdraw for a while. I wondered now how long she'd meant by a while. I even thought of calling her and asking her to help me figure out the difference between internal work and morbid depression but I didn't have health insurance anymore, let alone mental health insurance, and even if I had I couldn't bear the thought of going through it all again.

Maybe, I thought, as I drove out of the Subway parking lot, I just needed something else to do. Maybe I'd rested enough, gone on enough walks, drunk enough tea, taken enough naps. Maybe it was time to get back to work. When I got home I called Stan and said I'd start the following Monday. Great, he said, and we worked out a plan for three days a week.

I felt better after talking to Stan so I called my father and invited him for Sunday dinner—he came every week but he liked to be invited. I planned to tell him over dinner that I'd taken a job as a veterinary assistant and dog whisperer. I wasn't sure how to explain it after painting such a rosy picture of how well my freelance business was going but maybe he wouldn't ask too many questions. I'd noticed lately he cared less and less about what my sister and I did. He still liked to brag about Susan's successes but his time for regret and outrage over our failures and bad choices, mine primarily, was long past. Still, he could be momentarily riled up into some shadow of his former disapproving self, and I didn't feel up to his insults.

That Sunday I made a big pot of chili in the morning, early enough for it to stew all day and large enough that I could send most of it home with him. I used red beans and wild rice, which makes it chewy and slightly nutty, and the more beans and rice I use the less meat I need. I cook it in a sweet vinegar and tomato sauce with extra brown sugar and serve it with sour cream and chopped green onions. As I ladled it into our bowls that afternoon I mentioned I'd taken a new job and he was so distracted by the food he only grunted and nodded at the news.

"Bob's alma mater," he said when I told him the name of the shelter and then "pass that sour cream, would you? This is mighty good." He loved dairy products. He swore they were the secret to his longevity.

Chili for Consolation

Sauté a small finely chopped onion in olive oil. When the onion is transparent or nearly so add minced garlic, a clove or 2 to taste, and turn the heat way down immediately.

Add about ¾ of a pound of ground beef to the pan. Use the kind with some fat in it. Or if you do use lean beef and find the chili doesn't taste right, you can correct it by frying up some bacon on the side and crumbling that in at the end. Make sure it's crisp, though. Cook the beef fully.

Add 2 12-ounce bottles of Jewel brand chili sauce. I used to make my own but about a year ago I was at the grocery store shopping for chili supplies and studying various bottles of sauce, reading the ingredient lists and wondering whether I should make my own or just buy one ready made, when a strange man appeared behind me—I came to think of him as the chili angel—and handed me the store brand bottle. "This stuff is great," he said. "And it's cheap." So I bought it and he was right and now I always use that. Sometimes it's best to accept the kindness of strangers.

Add a can of kidney beans

Add ¼ cup vinegar, less if you like it sweet

Add ¼ cup brown sugar

Add 2 cups of wild rice. Did you know that wild rice is not even rice but seagrass and that the Plains Indians used to harvest it by paddling their canoes alongside the tall grasses in the rivers of Wisconsin and tapping them with their paddles so the kernels would fall into their boats? This is such a beautiful story that I eat wild rice whenever I have a chance. It lends a satisfying chewiness to chili, a kind of dark mystery. But always remember to add an equal amount of water, or a mix of water and red wine, or else the chili will be too chewy, especially if you're cooking for an old man with loose teeth.

Add cumin and hot pepper or pre-made chili seasoning.

Cook it on low for an hour or so and then turn off the stove and let it sit all day.

I serve it with tortilla chips on the side. Fritos also work.

Chapter 23

Po / Splitting Apart

Do not attempt to intervene now.

I like to count things. I look forward to it when I go to bed at night. I count to put myself to sleep or to distract myself from unpleasant circumstances. Sometimes I make a list and then count the items on the list and break it down into smaller lists and figure out what the percentages are of one to the other. I'll make a list of all the friends, business contacts or acquaintances I've spoken with on the phone or via email over a week's time and then I list those with dogs, those with cats, those with both and those with none. Then I figure out what percentage of my regular phone and email contacts has pets (sixty-two percent). I list friends I've spoken with in the past month who are in a relationship (eighteen), friends who are gay (four), friends who are divorced (eight), friends with children (three), friends who have been inside my house in the past month (exactly one), people I've spoken with in the past week that I know by name who color their hair (eleven, all women). It is soothing and eventually it puts me to sleep, usually quickly.

I make lists in my head of everything I ate that day or of every lunch or dinner I can remember eating in backwards order, starting from now. Usually I can go back a week or so. I list the seven deadly sins (anger, sloth, gluttony, avarice, pride, envy, lust) and how many I've committed that day. I list the five classes of vertebrate animals (mammals, birds, amphibians, reptiles, fish) and the five freedoms guaranteed by the first amendment to the Constitution (freedom of speech, freedom of the press, freedom of assembly, freedom of religion, freedom to petition to redress grievances.) I list the number of men I've slept with (eleven), the number of foreign countries I've visited (fourteen) and the number of cars I've owned (five). If that doesn't do it I list the thirty-one children who were in my eighth grade class by first and last name and if I still can't sleep I get up and drink another glass of wine. Then I count how many glasses of wine I've drunk that week.

I told Donna about this one time when she noticed me silently counting on my fingers. I was adding up how many yellow things she had in her kitchen and planning to compare it to how many I had in mine when I got home. She had twenty-seven, counting various boxes of cleaning products and the Paws for Love T-shirt she was wearing.

"There are drugs for that you know," she said.

"I know."

"Maybe you should go back into therapy, with the Phillip thing and all."

"Maybe," I said not looking up. I was slicing a banana for a fruit salad with a knife that had a handle in the shape of a lemon. "I kind of like things the way they are."

"Uh huh," she said disapprovingly. "Right."

Sometimes I felt like I was one of Donna's charity cases, like her battered women and bulimic teenaged girls. I'd met her in high school and even then she'd tried to get me to join more clubs. Donna believed in progress and improvement, in being busy, and there had been times I'd had to physically restrain her from cleaning my house. When she saw what she considered a problem she figured it was her business to fix it even if the problem was a person who didn't want to be fixed. She didn't believe in stillness. To her, anybody who wasn't on a self-improvement crusade seemed like a slacker and she was losing patience with me. I reminded myself not to count on my fingers anymore in her presence.

The night before the morning I started my new job, I couldn't sleep. I made a list of all the dogs' names I could remember from the clinic and then broke them into two groups, those with human names and those with cute or made-up names. I usually try to keep the list-making in my head but there were so many I had to turn on the light and write them down. I came up with forty-two human names and fifty-seven cute or made-up ones but some were judgment calls. Kumbaya for instance or Katmandu. Were these proper names or cute names? What about the yellow lab named Alana Banana? When I still couldn't go to sleep I made a list of all the things I could think of that I'd ever done for money and then I grouped them into four categories: useless and unpleasant (selling magazine subscriptions over the phone, my product development job for the last eight years), useless but fun (modeling for a drawing class in college wearing nothing but an orange batik scarf, my product development job for the first two years), useful but unpleasant (babysitting, waitressing) and both useful and fun (I could only think of one: working for Stan). Then I fell asleep and didn't wake up again until four-thirty in the morning when Clement floated onto the bed and meowed loudly to let me know his bowl was empty.

CHAPTER 24

Fu / Return

A time of darkness comes to a close.

I arrived twenty minutes early but Stan was already there. He handed me some paperwork to fill out.

"It's for taxes and insurance and all that crap," he said. Before he'd just paid me in cash.

"Insurance? Really?"

"Yeah. No dental though or mental health, sorry. You need it don't you? Insurance, I mean."

"Yeah. Thanks." It hadn't occurred to me I'd get health insurance. I'd let mine lapse when I quit my job and kept meaning to sign up but it was too expensive.

I shot him a look to let him know I meant it.

His answer got lost in his beard as he turned his attention to a scrawny, newly abandoned beagle puppy that had already escaped from his temporary carrying cage. The dog emitted a faint ammonia odor as he skittered across the waiting room floor dropping wet little turds behind him as he ran.

Stan pulled two pair of rubber gloves out of his pocket, snapped one pair on his hands and tossed the other in my direction.

"Welcome to my world," he said and began picking up the turds.

CHAPTER 25

Wu Wang / Innocence (The Unexpected)

All good comes when we are innocent.

When I returned from my first full day at the clinic, after listening to complaints and endearments from at least forty dogs and after a first lesson in how to give shots, there was a message on my answering machine from my father who'd called me that afternoon and wanted to talk. He rarely left messages—he was suspicious of answering machines and insulted by their bossy tone—so I knew it must be important.

I poured a glass of wine before I called him back.

He got right to the point. He'd been to see the doctor who had diagnosed him with what my father called "a case of the cancer." He wouldn't say what kind. Apparently his doctor had been monitoring him for some time though my father had not told me this either. They had already discussed treatment options—he was adamantly opposed to surgery. And chemotherapy. He had decided on a course of radiation against the advice of a team of doctors who had reviewed the case and said it was the least invasive but also the least effective treatment.

"That's great, Dad!" I said, entirely skipping over the bad news, refusing even to acknowledge it. "I mean. . . ." I tried to think of what I meant. The kitchen floor seemed to tilt sideways so I sat down on it. "I mean. It's great that it's controllable. And that there's a non-invasive treatment. Right?"

"Treatment schmeatment, my ass." He was shouting even louder than usual. "He says it won't work, the lowdown scoundrel. We'll see about that. That bastard had the nerve to tell me it would kill me."

"Well, he's just trying to help," I said, weakly.

"Oh bullshit. The bastard. The moron. The fat-ass schtunk. Bah humbug."

I was still on the floor, stirring patterns in the fallen crumbs and dog hair. I could just reach the counter for the wine and I poured another glass. We were in difficult territory now. My father resented the suggestion that he might die, ever, of anything. He expected me to agree and not to bring it up so I didn't and it was a shock to us both when someone else did. As soon as I could I shifted the conversation to the two-for-one sale on pork roast at Happy Foods, which cheered him up, and we ended there but not before he advised me not to get tricked into buying their over-priced milk.

There was a lot to think about. For one thing my father had cancer and the doctor had told him it would kill him, though he wouldn't say when. For another, my foster dog had diagnosed it. I tried to stay calm and concentrate on the higher laws and there-fore acquire the power that lay under them, as the *I Ching* had told me to do that morning. The only laws that seemed obvious though were that cancer trumped dairy product intake and that dogs knew a lot more than they let on.

I whistled Harvey over from where he and Bob and Gregoire had been lying in a pile. Bob sat up into his noble lion position, watching me closely while Greg stayed prone, thumping his tail and staring dreamily off into space. Harvey ran a couple of circles around the room before I caught him. I squeezed his ears and brought his whiskery face up close to mine, looking into his dark eyes for a sign of the intelligence that had sensed my father's ill-ness. We stared at each other for a moment and then he licked my mouth, hoping for food but getting only wine. I wondered what else he knew, what else they all knew. Maybe it was a blessing they didn't talk.

So much is made of the sweetness of dogs, and their good-ness is undeniable, but I wondered sometimes, if they could speak if we'd love them as much as we do in their silence. Maybe they'd tell us things we didn't want to hear and not just about our health. Probably they would. If they could diagnose faults in the physical body what character flaws and mental defects might they be privy to as well? I wondered. I kissed Harvey on his wet leather nose and let him go. He wasn't giving up any more secrets, not tonight at least. It was like releasing a spring. He bounced up and skidded across the kitchen floor then dashed over to gobble from Bob's bowl. A minute later Bob heaved himself up and, with toenails clicking on the linoleum, plodded sleepily toward his own bowl and firmly dislodged Harvey with one throaty exhalation and a shoulder nudge. Harvey may have been a young diagnostic genius but Bob ran the house.

CHAPTER 26

Ta Ch'u / The Taming Power of the Great

In the face of rising tension, keep still.
Honor in practice what you have learned
from the I Ching.

The next day I wasn't scheduled at the clinic and had planned to spend the morning working on my freelance projects. I was rewriting poems someone else had written for Administrative Assistants' Day plates. Rewrites were usually easy assignments with just a tweak here and there but I was stuck on the verse, written by a certain officious ex-colleague of mine. *Lord let me make a difference in everything I do, it's the little things that mean the most and shine back up at You.* It sounded like her all right, snotty and condescending, written as it was in the fake voice of the administrative assistant, presuming her sense of service in small acts. Why not just thank her? And the Lord part had to go—no way could you assume all the secretaries and their bosses were pious Christians who prayed to the Lord to be better employees. When I worked there I'd gotten into a habitual praise the Lord mode after working on so many religious products but from a little distance it seemed offensive. I tried a direct thank you: *You always make a difference in everything you do, for little things and big ones, blah blah blah thank you.* The problem with that was that it sounded too much like a greeting card. Why buy a thirty-dollar plate when you can send the same message on a two-dollar card and still afford flowers? It needed philosophy, beauty; it needed work.

I needed a distraction. I thought about calling Stan to thank him again for giving me health insurance and to tell him about Harvey's prescient sniffing, just to take the pressure off the poetry but decided not to. It wouldn't be news to him and I wanted to think it over for a while. Instead, after an unproductive hour writing in little timed spurts I gave up and packed the dogs into my car to head to the big dog park. Diane had left a message saying they were back—paperwork glitch, baby still not available—and I could drop Gregoire off anytime or she'd pick him up tomorrow. I knew what she meant by tomorrow; she wouldn't get around to it for days so I thought I'd take him for one more outing and then drop him at Diane's on my way back.

The big dog park is a thirty-acre parcel of land donated to the city by an elderly heiress who designated it for dog-friendly use only, prohibiting development in perpetuity. She kept the big stone house and surrounding gardens, which are visible through the brush as you walk the park, and sometimes in the winter when the leaves were off the trees I could see a tiny figure on the broad front porch and hoped it was her soaking up the dog gratitude vibes as she sipped her afternoon sherry and slowly glided into the afterlife. The rest of the estate belonged to the dogs and I went as often as I could.

Bob always knew where we were going when we got in the car. He muscled his way into the front seat, his eyes open unnaturally wide, leaning forward like a figurehead on a ship as if to speed the journey.

Gregoire, who had been on many dog park trips with us, cried in the back seat until I opened the window for him. His was a high simpering cry and the first time I heard it I thought he was suffering from some acute problem. Then I realized he just wanted fresh air to sniff. Gregoire was one of those earthly beings that suffered deeply over the smallest of problems. When humans acted the way Gregoire did I resented it, even when their suffering was clearly real to them. In Gregoire's case I was not even tempted to pass judgment. I didn't care how minor his ailment was; I didn't want him to spend one sorrowful moment on this earth. So I opened the back window and instantly he was happy again, a crying baby consoled by the smallest distraction. He stuck his head out, squinted his already beady collie eyes and fell into a contented silence while his glamorous fur blew back in the wind like the hair of a girl in a shampoo commercial. Harvey rushed back and forth on the back seat until I opened his window too. Then peace prevailed. We were on our way.

The dog park is a good place to think, even to approach a state something like peace if you don't mind barking and dog shit and the occasional bloody fight. As I walked down the path a flowing mass of dogs of all sizes and colors surged around me, an ocean of dogs, and my three blended with the rest, rushing off to play, to chase, to sniff and then returning for a pat on the head and a quick bit of eye contact. Occasionally a dog even larger than Bob, a Swiss Mountain dog or a full blooded mastiff, would approach him bossily and sniff his ass as if he had a right to and the hackles would rise along Bob's spine and he would growl and lunge for the other dog and I'd have to yell at him "Down, boy!" and grab him by the hips and drag him away. But it was all show on both our parts. He was defending his sense of himself as the biggest dog and I had to pretend I would and could keep him from fighting.

He wasn't a fighter though; he was a gentleman poseur, saving face with a threatening snarl but ultimately opting for peace. He always ended these skirmishes by looking mildly over his shoulder at me, smiling a little and then trotting to my side, pretending obedience when he was really just smart and sweet and did exactly as he pleased. My loyal boyo. I patted his head and relied on his good judgment. I preferred loyalty to obedience in dogs and men. Loyalty was a choice. Obedience was just a by-product of fear.

We made our way past the pond into a field of cattails. Bob trotted ceremoniously by my side while Gregoire and Harvey bounded through the prairie grass, charging other dogs and running figure eights around each other. Gregoire collected enough burrs in his coat in a ten-minute romp to require an hour of brushing later. I didn't worry—I'd yank out as many as I could and knew that Diane would just take him to the groomer after I left no matter what condition he arrived in. The dogs circled and greeted other dogs and sometimes jumped on their owners. No one minded; that's what everybody came for.

So when Harvey charged up to a small woman with coarse gray hair in a grown-out buzz cut, jumped up and stuck his head inside her maroon windbreaker, I didn't pay much attention. He sprang away, did a quick play bow in her direction and raced back, placing his paws on her chest this time and laying his head between her breasts.

I whistled him back and grabbed his collar. "Sorry," I called to her as I passed. She waved dismissively—no problem—though she didn't smile. Nobody came out here expecting to stay clean.

As I dragged him away Harvey craned his neck to look back at her. She had turned and was trudging stiffly toward the parking lot now behind a grimy Pomeranian in a pink rhinestone collar that glinted from under the dense mat of his orange fur. Harvey twisted around and stared at me: "Sick smell," he telegraphed.

"Me?" I said out loud.

He looked back at the woman, straining to get out of my grasp. "No, her. Sick," he said again, decisively this time.

Clearly he meant the tired-looking woman in the maroon windbreaker. Now what, I wondered. What was I supposed to do? Tell her? Tell her what? We kept walking. Which was the appropriate action here: yin or yang? Letting it go or intervening? Was this a let-me-make-a-difference moment or a going-with-the-*I-Ching*-passive-flow-of beautiful-acceptance moment? What would Jesus do? I knew what Donna would do.

I walked on for a while and then rallied the dogs and circled back. If she was still there when I got to the parking lot, I decided, I'd tell her. If not, the decision had been made for me.

But the woman was slow and when I got to the parking lot she was still making her way toward her car, now carrying the dirty orange fluff ball.

I piled my dogs into my car before I approached her.

"Excuse me," I called. She turned. She looked a little suspicious. "I know this may sound strange and I don't want to pry, but." I smiled, hoping she'd smile back and make it easier but she didn't. "Well, my dog senses things? Sometimes? For instance, he detected my father's illness. I mean, he smelled him and I kind of know how to read him? And then he, my father, went to the doctor and he was diagnosed. Um. With cancer. What I'm getting at is that he seemed to have a similar reaction to you. When he put his head on your um chest."

I grimaced, making my face into an apologetic mask. I had no idea how someone would take such an announcement or how I was supposed to act but I'd done my job. I wished I could just send her a letter and I half hoped she thought I was crazy. No wonder doctors are so wooden in their communications with patients, I thought, but at least they're not translating dog diagnoses.

"I'm sorry if this seems rude. I just thought I should tell you," I added lamely when she didn't reply. She was fumbling with her car keys and looked up. Her eyes were surprisingly blue and clear in an otherwise ruined face.

"Yeah, tell me about it," she said in a raspy voice. "I finished chemo about a month ago. My hair's coming back at least." She patted her buzz cut, "if not my energy."

She didn't seem offended or even particularly surprised.

"Thanks, though." She smiled crookedly, revealing a mouthful of horrible teeth. Then she gave a small wave, wafting the scent of stale tobacco in my direction as she climbed into her rusty maroon car.

Chapter 27

I / The Corners of the Mouth (Providing Nourishment)

Give proper nourishment to yourself and others.

After parking on a side street and yanking as many of the burrs out of his coat as I could, I dropped Gregoire off at Diane's house; she was at her yoga class so I handed him over to Juanita, the baby sitter. He had whimpered and looked accusingly at me with his slightly cross-eyed milk chocolate gaze as I pulled out the burrs. No telepathy was necessary; the simultaneous messages were clear: you're hurting me; I forgive you. He was a high-maintenance person, a problem child. I had guiltily looked forward to taking him home, now I already missed him. There still was Harvey though. I wondered how long I'd get to keep him before he was deemed civilized enough to be put up for adoption. He'd have to be placed carefully; his diagnostic talents or at least his habit of ambushing people and shoving his nose into their private parts wouldn't make him an instantly popular pet.

When I got home, I made four peanut butter and jelly sandwiches, two for me and one for each of the dogs (Clement only joined us for lunch when we had sardines), and settled down at the kitchen table with three nickels and my tea-stained copy of the *I Ching*.

I threw Po/Splitting Apart. *Do not attempt to intervene now.* I wondered if it was a reprimand for what had just happened at the park or if it meant not to intervene from now on. The *I Ching* was very much against social activism or any form of going against the flow. I read the explanatory text, which, as usual, cautioned in favor of patient nonaction in the face of adversity.

What did this mean exactly? Should the woman with the Pomeranian not take treatment for cancer? If she had not known she was sick should I not have told her? And what of me? Should I not intervene in my own life? Was my life not inactive enough already? It had shrunk in the past months, I had to admit. Was this life of small moves and small thoughts purposeful or simply passive; was it patient nonaction or creeping inertia veering toward madness?

There were some actions you really had to take and I proceeded to take them. I brushed my teeth. I washed the lunch dishes. I swept the floor. I called my father but no one answered. I left a message asking if he wanted me to do some grocery shopping for him. I wiped down the counters and made tea. I filled Clement's food dish with crunchy ocean feast. I changed the water in all the animals' bowls and I brought in the mail. Then I went back to my desk and set the kitchen timer.

The Administrative Assistants' Day poems still needed work. *Sometimes life seems worn with care / It's then that small things mean a lot / Sometimes they matter most of all / So thanks for giving all you've got!*

I felt a little sick. Maybe peanut butter didn't agree with me. The poems were meant to appear in the middle of wreaths of flowers, with a different poem for each seasonal flower arrangement. I dreaded sending in a sentiment like this—not only was it even more trite than usual but some clever person in the office might match the minimalist sentiment to my waning attention toward business in my last months there and was bound to make a joke of it. Small things indeed, this seemed to be all I did anymore. Smaller and smaller.

The buzzer rang on the kitchen timer and as it buzzed the phone rang too.

It was my father returning my call to say that he wouldn't mind a little help shopping today if I was planning to be in the area since he was feeling a little blue. His expression, blue. It was his way of saying he was tired all the time these days.

He kept a running shopping list of what he needed on the kitchen table and I wrote it down as he shouted it to me over the phone:

1 box Little Debbie Ho Ho's
6 small Brussels sprouts—small!
1 chicken pot pie
1 gallon whole milk
1 bottle gin
1 bag house brand frozen French fries
1 24-roll pack single ply toilet paper—the cheap stuff!
2 plum tomatoes
1 quart container cottage cheese, small curd
1 box house brand corn flakes
1 small head iceberg lettuce
1 small cabbage—very small!
1½ gallon vanilla ice cream—house brand! cheap!
1 can corned beef hash
1 package English muffins—house brand!
2 Snickers bars
2 books of postage stamps
1 attractive greeting card—with no text!
jar dark molasses

CHAPTER 28

Ta Kuo / Preponderance of the Great

*There are great pressures at work. By meeting them with
modesty and patience, you avoid misfortune
and meet with success.*

Paying attention: what if that was my real job I wondered as I
drove back from my father's house, having delivered the groceries,
done the laundry and submitted to his grumbling over my failure
to get the best price on toilet paper. He lay on the couch under a
pile of blankets. I held up each item to show him what I'd bought
and then I put it away where he told me. A misfiled can of corned
beef hash might never be found. What if that was all I or anyone
was really required to do? Pay attention. Be kind. Do no harm.
What if the yogis and the poets, the real ones not the plate poets,
were right and the dreamy dozing dogs were the models of correct living? It sounded easy, a matter of taking walks and going to
museums, releasing me, us all, from the tyranny of achievement
and the pursuit of wealth, released us all from Donna's plan to
change the world. What if right living *was* what it took to change
the world?

How we'd get goods and services I didn't know. Who would
make the paintings to hang in the museums or harvest the tea
to drink while we contemplated our breath? Who would make the
Little Debbie Ho Ho's my father loved to eat? I didn't know. Maybe
some people would want to work, feel a karmic call to work while
the rest of us just paid attention. It didn't make sense though. It
didn't add up.

Even if this was so, I wasn't doing a very good job, even
of that. The pain and price of starting to pay attention is the

awareness of how much we have already missed and how much we will miss every moment even if starting now we stayed awake and aware every second until we dropped dead. So much of my life had already been spent looking the other way from what I was doing, going to my job and sitting at a desk staring at the phone waiting for it to ring or hoping that it wouldn't, going to meetings and ignoring what was being said, while instead making lists in my head of places I'd rather be— Katmandu, Starved Rock, the Ring of Kerry, home in bed with a novel or a strange man. I had paid so little attention to so much of my life that most of my memories were not of things I'd done but of fantasies of what I'd imagined doing. In fact I had tried not to pay attention, living instead in a private dream of what else might happen. Part of me hated the thought of giving that up.

I thought of Mr. Payne, my eighth grade English teacher, and of a particular dreary March afternoon, the sound of the hissing radiator and the dank lettuce smell of the uneaten bologna sandwich rotting in a greasy brown paper bag in some-one's nearby desk. I thought of Mr. Payne, with his rounded shoulders and collapsed chest, perched on the edge of a child-sized desk as he stared out the tall schoolroom windows in that gray after-noon light which fell so dimly on his pilled gray sweater. It was the sad stage for our daily, morose literature class. In this light the skin on Mr. Payne's face looked like a much-used brown paper bag, the kind we carried our smelly lunches in, that had been balled up and then roughly smoothed out a hundred times, a creased map of a thousand roads all leading nowhere. He wasn't that old, about my age now, but to us he seemed ancient. Always in my memory he is as he was that bleak afternoon, perching one cheek of his droopy ass on a desk and quoting Milton to a class-room of thirteen-year-olds.

"When I consider how my light is spent / Ere half my days, in this dark world and wide," he intoned, sadly marking the beats of the iambic pentameter with his chopping right hand, his jowls trembling slightly. He went on. I don't remember most of it now but I do remember the ending:

> "God doth not need
> Either man's work or his own gifts; who best
> Bear his mild yoke, they serve Him best. His state
> Is kingly. Thousands at His bidding speed
> And post o'er land and ocean without rest:
> They also serve who only stand and wait."

Dramatic pause. Then, more softly he repeated the last line, "They also serve who only stand and wait."

Were those tears of defeat in his pale rheumy eyes as he looked right at me? Yes, tears! I saw them! Was this mere drama or real tragedy? And how dare he allow himself this extravagance of emotion in our presence, we who thought mainly about bras and boners? Surely he didn't suppose we'd understand.

But it wasn't we, it was me he looked at and he was right. I did understand. Maybe the only odd thing that dreary afternoon was that instead of finding it creepy or funny I already knew exactly how he felt. Unlucky me, I had the gift to foresee my own dim future in his lost self. I knew how Mr. Payne felt, waiting for something important to happen that would never happen. He wanted to believe that he also served as he read us poems and taught us how to diagram sentences but he didn't believe it for a minute and neither did I. None of us did. Yet to me his disillusion had seemed noble, attractive, romantic even. I hung on every word, every tear. For of course I loved him and more than tolerated his odd-tasting kisses in the cloak room after extra credit poetry sessions despite the stale tobacco-smelling grandfatherly cardigans that hung from his stooped shoulders.

I wondered though. Maybe, almost forty years later, it wasn't too disloyal to let it go. Maybe it was time to let the romance of Mr. Payne's poetic anguish rest in peace. Maybe all I had to do was to live like a dog in a happy body, enjoying the curious smells of the world around me.

CHAPTER 29

K'an The Abysmal (Water)

Flow like pure water through difficult situations.

The next morning when I got to the clinic Stan asked if I thought Harvey was ready to be put up for adoption. I said that he was housetrained, could now walk on a leash without jumping, could sit and stay on command and had proven himself able to live with a cat and other dogs and to interact respectfully with a frail old man. He was quite civilized, I pointed out, except that he went wild when he smelled someone's sickness.

He suggested I bring him in next time and said he'd see what he could do about placing him. In the meantime he said he had an odd case he wanted me to look at.

The dog, Grace, was some kind of mixed breed lap dog, about twenty pounds, blonde faded to gray, with a long bushy tail and floppy hair over her eyes like overgrown bangs. The hair around her mouth looked like a man's beard and framed a little mouth with pink lips and sharp teeth. She wore the sour facial expression of a chronically disappointed human. She'd probably been cute when she was groomed and young. The same could be said for me, I supposed, but now she was matted, unkempt and unloved-looking. And she smelled bad.

Grace growled when Stan approached her cage; she trembled and leaked a little urine as we entered.

"She was dropped off a couple of days ago by a guy who said she'd bitten his grandkid. His wife wanted her put down. I don't think he had the heart to make the decision or he figured we'd do it. She's eleven. They had her since she was a puppy."

I thought of what terrible things Donna would have said at this point but I kept quiet. Stan said he wanted me to spend time with her and tell him what I thought.

"Be careful of your face and wear these," he said, handing me some thick greasy gloves. "In case she bites."

He snapped a pink nylon leash on her collar and handed me the loop end. Then he headed off to his office.

Grace skittered off ahead of me toward the door and I walked her around the yard. It was a gray day with a little mist in the air. Grace was well upholstered and I didn't worry about taking her outside. Fresh air and a walk would do us both good.

We headed over to a bench and I sat down. She stood next to it and made a low snoring sound in her throat. I patted the seat of the bench and after a couple of ineffectual lunges she sat down on her haunches and started to grunt and whine. She was a noisy little thing and smelly, even outside; there was probably feces stuck in her matted coat. They hadn't gotten around to giving her a full bath and haircut yet. Maybe they didn't bother with it if they planned to put a dog down.

The bench wasn't that high but she couldn't make the leap so I grabbed her around her barrel chest and boosted her up. She snarled and tried to nip my hand but the thick glove was impervious. When I didn't react to being nipped the growling subsided and finally she relaxed a little though her eyes were wild and she still made the snoring sound.

We sat in relative silence for a while and then I said, out loud, "So, I hear you bit some kid."

She looked over at me, her round bloodshot little eyes strangely light for a dog. She looked very human. The remnants of a dingy pink ribbon were stuck in her matted topknot.

No reply. We stared at each other. *Why did you do that?* I didn't bother to say it out loud. I could tell by the way she was looking at me she knew what I was talking about.

He stuck a spoon up my ass.

That's terrible, I said. I meant it.

They kept me in a cage all the time.

That's awful, I said.

They never let me outside. I was in a cage with my own shit.

I'm so sorry.

I want a bath and I want to get out of here, she said.

Are you going to keep biting people?

Yes.

I looked away.

Be nice to me.

I looked back at her. "OK. I can do that," I said it out loud. She let me reach over and scratch her behind the ear. She made a sound in the back of her throat like a coffee pot.

Be nice and keep your distance, she said.

But she let me pet her.

CHAPTER 30

Li / The Clinging (Fire)

Cling to the power of higher truth.

Stan called me that night to say that after I left she bit the nurse. She was old, he said, nobody wanted her and she bites. And she had kidney disease. They were going to put her down.

"I thought it was a no-kill place."

"Not for incorrigibles."

"Come on. Who ever heard of an incorrigible Westie?"

"It's for the best, Maryanne. You want her living here in a cage for the rest of her life? Nobody touching her, ever, because they're afraid of her? That's what her life would be. We can't adopt her out—you have to tell people these things. Nobody'd want her. She's eleven years old, she's ill and she bites."

I didn't say anything.

"Not even you, Maryanne. Be honest. And don't volunteer because I'm not giving her to you."

"But it's their fault," I said. "You know it is. After eleven years."

"Maybe. Who knows."

The next morning there was an email requesting five more verses, now for Administrative Assistants' Day commemorative jewelry. They'd changed it to pendants, which were to be etched on the back. Each one was supposed to mention the name of a flower—rose, lily, forget-me-not. And could I say something about the symbolism of each flower? I clicked on keep as new. If my boss called I'd pretend I hadn't seen it yet. I called Stan.

"Did you do it yet?"

"What? Oh. Not yet, soon."

"Let me come."

"Are you crazy."

"Probably. Would you just please wait. I'll be there in half an hour."

I put on a black T-shirt and a black sweatshirt, blue jeans and hiking boots, stuffed a handful of Milkbones in my pocket and grabbed a book from the shelf as I ran out to the car. I moved fast so I didn't have time to think about what I was doing.

Stan met me at the front desk and gestured with his head toward his examining room. His curly hair looked matted, as usual, as if he hadn't combed it yet that morning. The nurse, her hand bandaged, had already brought Grace in. She smelled. No one had gotten around to giving her a bath and now she was going to die smelling of her own shit. Her leash was clipped to a pole; she sat tensely on the examining table, her suspicious eyes following our movements. She stared at me. She knew exactly what was going on.

"Do you mind if I say something?"

"What? Oh." Stan looked suspiciously at the book I was holding. "You mean like a funeral?"

"It's short, please." I held my hand up like a crossing guard preventing children from venturing into the street. The dog was staring at me and I felt ridiculous. I also felt terrible discussing the protocol of the dog's death in front of her, as if she didn't know. Or as if I didn't know she knew.

Stan made a kind of wincing face but he took a step back, waving his hand in a way that looked like chivalry, a ladies first gesture meaning that I should step up next to the examining table. The little tray with the needles on it was on a table within reach.

Stan folded his hands in front of him and lowered his chin, sliding his eyes to look at me.

Was I embarrassed? Yes. I felt foolish to feel the emotion I felt, which was real grief. After all these months of being frozen finally I felt something, a great pressure on my chest and in my head, the pressure of real sorrow and something else even more painful.

"You are loved," I said as quietly as I could to the smelly little dog that at least had stopped growling. I passed a Milkbone under her nose. She ignored it, cheap bribe that it was, so I set it down by her feet.

She looked me in the eye and I waited for her to speak but she refused. Then I took her paw with my right hand; I stroked it and then crept my hand up to her ear and stroked there. Then, holding the book in my left hand, I read her a Mary Oliver poem, coming with relief to the line "each body a lion of courage, and something precious to the earth." It was all I remembered from having read it years ago and why I'd grabbed the book. It was the best I could do on the spur of the moment for the fierce little animal.

After I'd finished reading I stepped back and Stan took my place. He slid the first needle in and then when Grace closed her eyes he gave her the second shot. Soon she stopped breathing.

CHAPTER 31

Hsien / Influence (Wooing)

An influence comes. Good fortune to those
whose hearts are correct.

Twelve hours later Stan was sitting at my kitchen table. I'd invited him for dinner. So here he was, in clean khakis and a denim shirt, tweed jacket and running shoes. I'd never seen him dressed up before. Bob sprawled lion-like at his feet, solemnly glad to have a man at the table again. I stood at the counter slicing a cucumber for the salad, tossing a slice in Bob's direction. He opened his mouth and caught it on the fly without getting up.

Harvey trotted around the room, showing off the good manners that were supposed to earn him a permanent home. The plan was that Stan would evaluate his house-friendliness and if he deemed him well trained enough would take him back to the shelter at the end of the evening.

Death makes us crave company and food, even the death of a dog. We must eat together after a funeral, after the long vigil at the hospital bed. Neighbors arrive with casseroles, coffee cakes, hams on disposable tinfoil platters. As my mother lay dying refusing to eat, I returned from my visits to find Phillip cooking elaborate consoling meals, hearty and filling. He grilled steaks or fishes stuffed with herbs; he cooked big bowls of pasta with complex sauces. He even baked bread. I returned home one Saturday to find a row of fleshy pale bundles wrapped in dish towels lying on the radiator, our surrogate newborn babies: quadruplets. Food was life and the imminence of my mother's death reinforced the contrast, inspiring him to new culinary heights. The living eat, the dying don't; at the time it seemed as simple as that and maybe it always is.

After we'd killed Grace, Stan asked if I wanted him to pick up Harvey later that night and I said sure. Then I said why don't you stay for dinner and he said sure. I left the clinic and drove straight to the grocery store, composing a menu in the parking lot on the back of a six-month-old parking ticket.

Appetizers: olives, goat's cheese, garlic toast, and, what the hell, pâté. It was a funeral feast for Grace; pâté would honor her.

Main course, comfort food: roast chicken or pasta? Roast chicken with mashed potatoes would be my choice but I worried. Men seem embarrassed by mashed potatoes; they're too soft, too juvenile, too breast-like. Potato salad, then. Green beans, green salad. A raspberry pie. If we didn't eat the pie Bob and I would have it for breakfast the next day and I'd take the rest to my father.

After shopping I'd rushed home to clean the house. Or to rearrange things and mop up a couple of months' worth of paw prints from the kitchen floor and make sure there were no dirty sweat pants, or worse, on the couch. It was too late and too expensive to call a cleaning service. Housekeeping for me was event-driven, not something I did systematically or often. My mother had hired people to clean and so had Phillip who disapproved of the results when I attempted the job. I wasn't as helpless as he believed, just indifferent to dirt beyond food and bathing zones. Filth was relative I felt and I tended not to notice floors. But Stan's visit merited some sprucing up.

He arrived exactly on time with a bottle of Chianti. I was glad because I intended to drink. We toasted Grace. We ate the pâté and the cheeses. He admired Harvey's manners. After we finished the Chianti we opened a bottle of Shiraz. We ate the chicken and the potato salad and the beans.

The tension of the day, the warmth of the food, the wine had all made me a little drunk. I was making him tell me about putting animals to sleep.

"Do they suffer?"

"Absolutely not. That's the whole point of doing it. To end suffering when there's no hope it will end otherwise except in a slower death."

Bob had been lying quietly on the floor between us during this conversation, his alert face a furrowed map of concern. Now I could hear his thoughts clearly voiced in my own head. "It's a good thing, Maryanne," he said. "Don't give him a hard time. He's a nice guy."

He'd never interrupted a conversation before. I looked at him.

"Tell him you understand," he prompted.

"I suppose that's good then," I said, glancing at Bob. Now he was giving me orders.

"It's not my favorite part of the job," Stan said, sitting very straight in his chair and transferring a forkful of chicken breast to his mouth. He liked to eat and I liked this about him. He had dark green eyes under a heavy brow and a neat pink mouth in the middle of a precisely groomed mat of graying hair. He reminded me of a small handsome gorilla. Large amounts of food disappeared while I talked.

When I poured us both more wine I noticed Clement had joined us and was sitting somberly on the counter next to the bread box where he had formed himself into a compact shape resembling an orange bowling pin. His mouth was set in a little pink frown but curved up on the sides into a secret smile. He was listening.

"Don't you ever feel overwhelmed?" I said. "I mean by everything dying all the time? Don't you ever wonder how to deal with it, honor it?"

"You can't. You can't have funerals all the time," he said. "Although I liked what you did today." He ate some more potato salad. "I was thinking maybe." He picked up his wine glass.

"Maybe what?"

"Maybe we could do that once every couple of months for them all, for the ones who don't make it, along with the ones we have to put down. It's rough on the volunteers. I think they'd like it. It would make everybody feel better, just a short ceremony of some kind. It could be part of your job."

I hesitated.

"Tell him yes," said Bob.

"Sure, I could do that," I said.

I told him about my father. He told me about his eighty-one-year-old mother, Edith, who had taught fourth grade at St. Rita's Catholic School for twenty-three years and was now an Alzheimer's patient at an assisted living facility in Evanston, and about his daughter Julie, who was in med school at the University of Illinois. He told me about his ex-wife and I told him about Phillip, sort of, except I made it sound funny and like we were still friends. I didn't want to trash him in front of Bob. He saw through that.

"Shit happens," he said.

"That's for sure."

Stan declined pie and stood up, saying he needed to go. Two neat strips of chicken lay on his plate and he took one in each hand and fed them to the dogs.

He called Harvey over, snapped a leash on him and then swiftly, in one motion, as if leashing a dog were part of a larger choreography, leaned over and kissed my cheek, near my hair. The move was unexpectedly graceful.

"Thanks for dinner," Stan said.

Harvey trotted beside him as they headed down the path toward the street and then turned to look back at the three of us, Bob, Clement and me, standing in the porch light at the front door.

"Thanks," Harvey said. Bob barked in reply.

CHAPTER 32

Hêng / Duration

Remain steady and allow the world to shape itself.

Here is what I cooked for Stan.

Funeral Dinner in Honor of an Unloved Dog

Roast Chicken for Comfort

Rinse one 3-pound free-range roasting hen and coat it
with oil, salt, pepper and rosemary.

Free-range chickens, like free-range chicken eggs, are more
expensive. Some farms call their poultry—another nice distancing
euphemism—free-range but still breed the kind that can't walk.
What's the point of allowing chickens to roam if their legs won't
support them? Standing under the fluorescent grocery store light
I stared at the body parts of these chickens, both free-range and
no-range and considered the fact that we have figured out how to
create animals that only suffer until they die so they can be eaten
by us. It made me feel like a stone was pressing on my chest. Was
it right to honor the death of one animal by eating the flesh of
another? Though I knew that Grace had lived on kibble made from
lamb and chicken parts. And that if every death were marked with
honor life would be nothing but a series of funerals, earth nothing
but a graveyard.

"Who killed the pork chops?" Allen Ginsberg had Walt
Whitman demand in the supermarket poem. I picture the old man
with his long beard leaning over the cool shelf of meat, his face

lit from below by the fluorescence glinting off the plastic shrink wrap stretched over the pinkish chops. Were they both vegetarians? Either?

But I digress. Some of the most expensive chickens have a pleasing farm label on the packaging and when I've looked up the brand on Google it claims to have chickens that do range, that live lives before they give them up. This is the brand I buy; it costs two dollars per pound more than the other brand. I think if I make myself consider these things each time I buy meat, one day I won't want it anymore, but my appetite is alarmingly impervious to my better nature and so far I have not reached that point.

Chop up several cloves of garlic and 2 lemons and place in cavity. Body cavity: there's an expression that won't let you forget what you're eating.

Roast for about 30 minutes per pound plus another hour or so on low heat. Always cook a chicken for a long, long time. Cover with foil when the skin reaches the degree of golden brown crispness you prefer. It's not finished until the leg falls off when you jiggle it.

Potato Salad for Solace

Scrub and boil 4 medium red potatoes, cut in quarters. I leave the skin on for color and texture.

Boil them until they are just right. That means not too soft and not too hard. They shouldn't fall apart when you cut them into pieces. I have been cooking potatoes since I was nine but I do not know how long that takes. The cautious approach is to cook them 10 minutes or about halfway done and then turn off the stove and cover them. Go back and poke them now and then. Eventually they will get soft.

Drain, salt and put them in the fridge. When they're cool and firm chop them into bite-sized pieces and mix with the following:

1 chopped hard-boiled egg
1 or 2 stalks chopped celery
2 or 3 chopped green onions
1 chopped pickle
Fresh chopped dill
Mayonnaise to taste
A little white vinegar (avoid the others; they dye the
    potatoes unappetizing colors)
Salt and pepper
A moderate spoonful of Colman's powdered mustard

Mix it all up with a fork so that you don't smash the potatoes, and sprinkle chopped parsley or cilantro on top along with paprika.

Green Beans for Grief Relief
(lemon always cheers me up)

Wash and snap the tops off 1 pound plump green beans.

Place in a shallow bowl leaving a little water at the bottom.

Squeeze juice of one lemon over beans.

Crush one clove of garlic over beans.

Pour some olive oil over beans.

Microwave for 6–8 minutes.

Add salt and white pepper and toss.

Chapter 33

Tun / Retreat

This is a time for disengagement and retreat.
In stillness you are out of the reach of danger.

I slept late the next morning and when I awoke to full light there was Bob standing next to the bed, somberly tapping the mattress with one paw and staring intently into my eyes. This meant it was time for his walk, past time, and that he had to urinate.

I was exhausted from yesterday's events. I was not used to days so full. Death, housecleaning, cooking, rich food, conversation with a human, wine, even a hint of sex for what else was a good night kiss, even if it was on the cheek, in my limited world where not a single tender contact had passed between me and any man other than my father for over a year. Phillip had moved out only six months before but physical contact had ceased long before that. Had Stan intended the kiss to be seductive or just polite? Had I intended the dinner to be seductive or just friendly? How embarrassed should I feel? I wondered as I dragged Bob along his usual route at a pace slightly faster than he preferred. He looked up at me, aggrieved, then sat down in protest, his extra neck skin wrinkling up over his collar and around his face as I tugged at the leash, his eyebrows working themselves together into a hurt expression. When I didn't stop pulling he said, "Do you mind? Would you please just wait while I sniff this bush?"

"Sorry."

"You drink too much."

"I know but it's none of your business."

My head ached; Bob was right. I was hung over. I was determined to think of the dinner as friendly. Anything else was too complicated. At least, I thought, I had the whole day free and, despite Stan's admirable appetite, a refrigerator full of leftovers including a whole raspberry pie. I planned to do nothing but sleep and eat.

When I got home the phone was blinking. The message was from Stan's nurse Bonnie calling to say he was out unexpectedly today and could I fill in. I took two aspirin and called back.

"Fill in?" I shut my right eye—that felt better. I could see my reflection in the window of the microwave. I looked like a stroke victim, the whole right side of my face drooped. My teeth hurt and were still dark from the wine. "Bonnie, I'm no vet, I'm not even a nurse."

"I know, honey. Just help with routine stuff, make calls to cancel the appointments I can't handle. I can do some of it. Stan suggested I call you."

She'd employed the irresistible maternal "honey." I'd do anything for a woman of a certain age who called me honey.

"Sure, OK." Maybe I'd poisoned us both with too much garlic in the beans. It felt as though there were an eel inside my skull behind my right eye, forming itself into a fist to squeeze my optical nerve. I imagined that it exuded poison and was the color of raw chicken and that it had a pulse; as it beat I could feel my eye throb. The poison seemed to seep into my jaw. I tried to think of a cure—root canal, brain surgery, decapitation, sleep.

"So how soon can you be here?"

It took me two hours to get there—I allowed myself a bath— but I stayed until closing, at seven. As I was leaving Bonnie said Stan had just called, no change, he was going to be out tomorrow too. "Can you come back?"

Two days off for a hangover and embarrassment over a kiss on the cheek?

"I guess so. I mean sure. Of course, yes. Can I ask why he's out?"

"Oh, I thought he'd told you. His mother. She took a turn for the worse last night. He's there now; he's planning to stay. You know, until the end. They don't expect it to be long. But you never know."

Chapter 34

Ta Chuang / The Power of the Great

To achieve true power and true greatness
one must be in harmony with what is right.

Stan was out the rest of the week. His mother died Thursday night. I worked every day and whatever I'd been doing at home didn't seem to suffer for my not being there. My old boss left a message asking me to lay off the Administrative Assistants' Day poems for a while, saying they'd put that program on hold and would pay a kill fee for whatever I'd done so far. They were putting all their resources into sports promotions now, she said. That's where the money was. My overpowering need for an afternoon nap had disappeared completely.

Saturday morning I called Stan at home and left a message saying I was sorry to hear about his mother and that I planned to come in as usual on Monday. Then I put Bob in the car and headed out to the big dog park to make up for all the walks we'd missed that week.

When we got back two hours later, comfortably tired and with Bob's coat smelling of sunshine and mud, there were messages from my father, Donna and Stan.

I hit the speaker button and played the messages out loud. Both Bob and Clement liked to listen and now they gathered near the phone. My father wanted to know if he should bring the ham a neighbor had dropped off at his house when he came to dinner tomorrow. The ham, he said, was big enough to choke a horse.

Bob and Clement looked at each other.

Donna wanted to know if I'd compose a slogan for T-shirts for a fundraiser she was organizing for abused women and Stan wanted me to call him.

As I dialed Stan's number I wondered if there was some way I could work the Administrative Assistants' Day poems into a slogan for Donna. A woman answered and put Stan on. There was a commotion. "Let me go in the other room. My brother and his wife and their dogs are here. It's kind of a zoo. Thanks, Kay, I'm going to take this in here."

Stan sounded tired. He thanked me for working, thanked me for calling. Said he had one more favor to ask.

"I don't know, maybe I shouldn't even ask you this. And I definitely would pay you. But let me tell you what it is first and see if you'd be willing."

"What?"

"I liked what you did at the clinic for Grace."

Stan wanted me to help him plan a memorial service for his mother. He needed something that wouldn't offend his brother and his wife, who, he said, called themselves post-Christian practicing agnostics and were strongly opposed to a religious service. His mother's younger sister was very much alive and still a nominal Catholic.

"What did your mother want? You should do that."

"She wanted to be cremated but after that she didn't say. If we do something at a church it will feel phony to everyone except maybe my aunt. My mother never went much. I think she thought it was pretty much a crock though she never said so. But she wouldn't have wanted a fight."

"I think I can do this," I said. "Why don't you come over. You want your brother to come too?"

"God no," he said. "They're leaving today anyway. Coming back for the service in two weeks. I think if it were up to them they'd just want to drop the ashes in a dumpster and go out to lunch."

"I'll handle this," I said surprising myself. I sounded like Donna. "Have you eaten yet?"

Stan was at my kitchen table an hour later for a late lunch. I didn't bother to shop this time. I served what I had around—sardines, slightly stale French bread, cheese, tomatoes, sliced fruit and some of Phillip's Belgian beer that was still in the back of the refrigerator.

"Good beer," Stan said, glancing at the label and frowning as he suppressed a belch.

Grief didn't seem to affect his appetite. After we'd eaten we got down to work. In the time it had taken him to get there I'd planned a basic service, a list of questions and a couple of suggested readings.

CHAPTER 35

Chin / Progress

You progress like the rising sun.
The brighter your virtue, the higher you rise.

It used to be that people spoke to me of sex. Unbidden and often, friends and strangers confessed to me their secrets. They told me about their affairs and their desires as if seeking absolution. I of course had none to give. I had no advice for them, either, only questions. Now they speak to me of death in the same intimate tones.

Neighbors whose names I don't know come out of their houses to tell me their dogs have died. Women in the checkout line at the grocery store confide their sad anniversaries to me as we lay our frozen waffles and cucumbers side by side on the moving black belt. The boy was twelve, she says, and he died this day twenty-six years ago. They tell me as if I needed to know.

Maybe I did need to know. I realized as I sat down to work on Stan's mother's service that it felt natural, that it felt, in fact, like the most natural thing in the world.

After interviewing Stan a little, here's what I proposed: a simple outdoor ceremony consisting of readings at the end of which Edith's ashes would be scattered into the Chicago River. The ash dumping wasn't legal but the event would be so informal and the quantity of ashes so small I figured they could get away with it. The event would take place alongside the river just blocks from the octagon bungalow where Edith Barney, née Grabowski, had lived for forty-two years on a thirty-foot-wide city lot, first with her two sons and her husband Stanley, whose father had shortened the family name from Baranowski to Barney, and then alone after the sons moved out and Stan Sr. died. The site was where Stan remembered walking with his mother and his daughter, after the divorce, on awkward weekend custody visits with Julie, when she was still small. Edith had known what to do with the little girl, how to entertain her. Sometimes Stan had brought along Betsy too, a docile German shepherd who liked to swim.

After the simple ceremony I recommended a short hike along the river as a kind of walking meditation. A highway overpass had been built nearby; it was not an ideal place for a memorial service but it was where Stan remembered his mother had been happy or maybe just where he had been most at ease with her. And setting it outside would save him from awkward disagreements with his God-squeamish relatives. Then to lunch.

I suggested Stan send an email notifying invitees of the general plan so they would wear sensible shoes and suggesting they all meet in the parking lot nearby and hike down together. He started to scribble this down in a notebook but I told him I'd already written it all out. He looked up, his expression a mix of alarm and gratitude. "It's just a suggested text," I said to soften the intensity of it, "you can change it. Someone has to be the MC, though. You probably. Are you OK with that?"

Stan was hanging his head between his knees, his hands clasped. "OK. Unless you'd do it," he said.

"Not appropriate," I said, thinking of the pompous, clueless minister at my mother's grave. He'd never met her and if he had she wouldn't have liked him. "You might read a remembrance," I said. "Or just extemporize. You could read a poem or two, if you're comfortable with that? I have some suggestions here." I looked up to check his reaction. "OK, maybe not. How about Julie? She could speak. And your brother." Stan let out a big sigh at the mention of his brother.

"Then other people can say things. Tell them in advance so they're not taken by surprise. I've got it all written out for you."

Stan's elbows were still resting on his knees and his head still hung down in intense listening posture. He looked worried. I continued.

"After everyone's through speaking you'll allow a moment of silence. For those who pray. The others, well, too bad. They can use it to add up their expenses."

Stan had been staring at the floor and rubbing Bob's haunch with his toe in a circular motion. Now he looked up.

"Sorry. A brother joke," I said. "Then sprinkle the ashes. After that maybe Julie or whoever is the youngest can pass out wild-flowers and everyone can throw one into the river. No? Birdseed? Maybe birdseed is better. Some kind of communal act is nice."

I was remembering the oppressively sunny October day we'd buried my mother's ashes, months after her funeral. Better get them in before the ground freezes, we'd been told. It was just my father, Phillip and me. And the minister. Susan was giving a dinner party that week and couldn't make it. The minister was a barrel-chested, big-haired blowhard of a man in a tight beige suit with sweat stains under his arms and an overly sonorous voice. After we listened to him drone on about love, hope and faith we each shoveled a mound of dirt into the grave where the cemetery attendant had placed the urn containing my mother's ashes. My father had collected them from the funeral parlor that morning— the cremains they insisted on calling them—and carried the urn to the gravesite in a deluxe brown grocery bag with reinforced handles, one he'd saved for a special occasion. Afterward my father invited the minister to join us for lunch, and he'd followed us hopefully in his battered station wagon all the way back to the house for the chicken casserole my father had put in the oven that morning. The minister seemed disappointed. He thought we were taking him to a restaurant.

"Here are these," I said to Stan, handing him a sheaf of Mary Oliver poems I'd printed off the Internet. "In case you change your mind. I promise they're not religious." I shuffled through the papers. "Here's the one I read for Grace, about the bear."

I also wanted to recommend the verse I liked: *Love is strong as death* from the Song of Solomon but was afraid I was pushing it. Stan sat staring at the papers like a diligent student who had signed up for the wrong class but was determined to stick it out and try for a B.

I handed the whole package over to him and he picked up the stack wearily.

"Thanks. Wow. I need to think through the details but basically, yeah. Thank you."

At the door he turned around and said, "Oh I forgot. I want to pay you for this. It's such a load off my mind, I'm thinking. . . ."

"Don't be ridiculous."

I couldn't think of what else to say so I smiled and slammed the door on him in mid-sentence, waving goodbye through the window.

Here's the Mary Oliver poem:

WHEN DEATH COMES

When death comes
like the hungry bear in autumn
when death comes and takes all the bright coins from
    his purse

to buy me, and snaps his purse shut;
when death comes
like the measle pox;

when death comes
like an iceberg between the shoulder blades,

I want to step through the door full of curiosity, wondering;
what is it going to be like, that cottage of darkness?

And therefore I look upon everything
as a brotherhood and a sisterhood,
and I look upon time as no more than an idea,
and I consider eternity as another possibility,

and I think of each life as a flower, as common
as a field daisy, and as singular,

and each name a comfortable music in the mouth
tending as all music does, toward silence,

and each body a lion of courage, and something
precious to the earth.

When it's over, I want to say: all my life
I was a bride married to amazement.
I was a bridegroom, taking the world into my arms.

When it's over, I don't want to wonder
if I have made of my life something particular, and real.
I don't want to find myself sighing and frightened
or full of argument.

I don't want to end up simply having visited this world.

CHAPTER 36

Ming I / Darkening of the Light

Darkness reigns in the external world now.
Disengage from negative feelings and
maintain your inner light.

Stan's visit, or maybe it was the conversation about death, left me energized. I cleaned up the lunch dishes, took Bob for a walk along his favorite muddy route and then—it was now almost four o'clock—went back to my office to read over the script for the memorial service and fine-tune some details. I was remembering something from a funeral I'd attended a couple of years earlier that I wanted to include. In the midst of life we are in death. Something like that.

I sat down at my computer, fingers poised over the keys. The email icon was bouncing at the bottom of the screen: a distraction, a temptation, a nuisance, a test of my ability to concentrate. I looked to see who had sent it.

Phillip. We hadn't spoken in six months. The weekend he came back to move out his things, I'd arranged to be gone. Leaving the key under the doormat and the animals in Donna's care, I'd flown to New York for the weekend, not telling her or anyone else where I was going. I'd intended to look up a newly single old friend, male, but spent most of the time walking around the Natural History Museum looking at long-dead animals, and the rest of the time in bed in a cheap hotel room reading novels and eating room service food. I double-checked the email address. No question it was from him. The subject said "Long Time No Hear!"

I didn't have to open it now. I could open it tomorrow. Or never. Unopened it had a nice plump potential sitting there at the top of the email list like a destination on a map I might never visit but then again one which I might, a possibility I could entertain but never have to realize. If I left it unopened I could imagine all the nice things it might say. I'm sorry, for one, though that wasn't exactly what I wanted. Or let's get back together. Or I'm sending you a check for a large sum of money, though that wasn't it either. In fact I couldn't exactly focus on what I wished it would say. Maybe, I thought, I should wait to open it until I knew what I wanted it to say. Then I could will it to say that. According to Donna, who had observed this kind of behavior in me over the years, this was called magical thinking and, she implied, my downfall, a sign of emotional immaturity and not worth the time I put into it. But I wasn't so sure it didn't work. I tried very hard to imagine the best thing his email could say until the effort made me feel like I needed to lie down.

I lay in bed for a while with a back issue of *Dog Fancy* across my face, open to the centerfold on shelties, but I couldn't sleep. What I really wanted to do was to work on the memorial service for Stan's mother but all the energy for that had been drained by the sight of the bouncing email icon. I walked back to my office determined to ignore it and focus on my revisions. I sat down. I clicked on "Long Time No Hear!"

"Hi there!" it said. "How are you? I hope you're doing well. And how are those beautiful boys, still shedding like mad? Hopefully not too much. I'm OK, all things considered, and not shedding too much for an old guy. I know things were kind of rough when last we spoke but I hope you're feeling better now and I only wish the best for you. I'm in town staying with Linda and Pete, believe it or not. Remember Sid? Vicious? Well he finally croaked and guess who's in charge of the send-off. Anyway that's what I'm here for, and to clear out his stuff, etc.

The reason I'm writing is this: Do you want to have dinner? We could go to Charlie's for old time's sake or wherever you like. Pick someplace expensive—I'm buying. Love, Phillip."

I went back to the bedroom and lay down again. Then I returned to my office and reread the email. Love, Phillip? I clicked on reply.

"I'm fine," I typed. "Dinner at Charlie's sounds great. I haven't been there since the night you sent back the wine and we had to leave. I'm going to finish my steak this time no matter what. I'm free tonight, maybe not later in the week. Let me know." I clicked send and then opened the file labeled "Stan's Mother."

Sid was dead. I hadn't thought about Phillip's father in ages and now he was dead. Phillip and his sister Linda had taken to calling him Sid Vicious, or just Vicious for short, when the Sex Pistols' version of "My Way" came out, not for any physical resemblance to the singer but in reference to Sid's dyspeptic character and to the fact that "My Way" was his favorite song. For years he sang it weekly on open mic night at his favorite neighborhood tavern.

Ten minutes later another email appeared titled: "Cool!" It said "What time should I pick you up?"

Chia Jên / The Family (The Clan)

A healthy family, a healthy country, and a healthy
world—all grow outward from a single superior person.

I took a bath and washed my hair, blow-drying it into a shape I hoped would seem attractive. I needed a haircut. I put on a long black silky skirt with a slit up the side and a black yoga top and over that a cropped black cashmere sweater with an embroidered pink rose on the collar that I'd bought at the animal shelter thrift store where Donna volunteered. I tied a silk purple scarf around my waist as a belt. Put on an agate pendant in a sterling setting. Silver hoop earrings. Black sandals with chunky heels. I filed my toenails. I was eleven months overdue for a pedicure. I spit on a paper towel and polished dog park mud off the shoes. I assessed my hands: hopeless. Animal wrangling had roughened and nicked them. I lathered them with hand cream and filed my nails neat and short. Clear polish would have been better but I didn't have time; clean would have to do. I hadn't dressed up in months and I was rusty on the details. It occurred to me, guiltily, that Stan had never seen me in anything other than muddy hiking boots, torn jeans and denim shirts over industrial strength bras.

I still had time so I put on make-up. First I dabbed concealer over my wine-mottled, wind-burned skin, then added eyeliner, eyebrow pencil, pink lipstick. I considered mascara but decided against it: too risky. The doorbell rang promptly at seven o'clock; Phillip stood on the rattan welcome mat looking like a TV game show host and holding a bouquet of yellow tulips.

Kiss on the cheek. He tried to pull me in closer but I resisted and instead patted him firmly on the back, feeling an odd longing, not for him exactly but for the remembered feel and smell of his expensive Oxford blue shirts and the confident well-remunerated world they represented. I thought of Daisy Buchanan crying over Gatsby's shirts and for the first time I sort of understood. He was aglow, as usual, tan, perfectly pressed, perfectly tailored. His shoes shone. At the sight of his manicured hands I hid mine. His oddly intense turquoise blue eyes were the same. My mother was always impressed by how handsome Phillip was, surprised that I could attract such a man though she never said so outright. She would have been less surprised if she'd lived long enough to see him leave. Suddenly I remembered I'd forgotten to brush out Bob who at that moment came wobbling confusedly and then galloping wildly out of the bedroom where he'd been snoozing, his crooked stub of a tail wagging his whole body side to side, his mouth open in a rakish smile, ears pressed back in his most hopeful way, hopping up on his stiff hind legs in pure joy.

When he got to Phillip he let out a kind of half-human howl, the kind he reserved for the most extreme circumstances, and tried to jump up to place his front paws on Phillip's shoulders in a full body hug, a trick they'd perfected and used to perform for the amusement of dinner guests. Phillip was hoisting him up under the shoulders to help but Bob wasn't up to the stunt anymore; it was too hard on his joints. Bob yelped once in pain and then Phillip was down on the floor with him—his immaculate clothes, my dirty floor—with his arms around Bob's head whispering my boy my boy into the graying fur inside his ear.

I was glad I'd opted against mascara. I checked around for Clement. Cool Clement. He was sitting outside, in a corner of the porch, watching this scene impassively through the front window. He blinked once. "Give him my regards," he said and then slipped off into the bushes in the direction of his favorite sun-soaked patch of dirt. I took it as a sign of solidarity. Good boy.

"Clement's out for a walk I guess," I said. "I'm sorry. I didn't have a chance to round him up."

"It's OK," he said. Phillip looked seriously unbalanced. Bob could do that to someone.

"Charlie's then?" He was concentrating on brushing dog hair off his pants and tucking his shirt back in. There was drool on one expensive shoe.

"Sure," I said.

Bob watched from the front window as Phillip held the door of the rented BMW open for me. When he turned the key the radio came on loud, to NPR. We drove to Charlie's Bistro, formerly Charlie's Supper Club, in silence except for the sound of two architecture critics competing to see who could most wittily trash the new Trump Tower.

The place had the same hokey suburban hauteur mixed with lodge décor that I remembered—pine paneling, a wood fireplace blazing in every season, white linen table cloths, a sommelier in a slightly greasy jacket. It was a never-updated, decades-old vision of elegance, the name change their sole concession to modernity. We'd started going there as a joke, the so-unhip-it-was-hip alternative to our city hangouts when we'd first moved here. We'd made fun of it but the parking was free and the food was good. After years of loyal attendance at our favorite BYOB Vietnamese restaurant on Argyle Street, the one with the dingy interior, the cockroaches and the incomparable shrimp and basil spring rolls, we'd gone suburban and settled on this as our default special occasion place.

We both ordered steaks, medium rare. He picked an expensive Cabernet from the wine list.

"I'm sorry about your dad," I said.

"Thanks," he said. "You're looking well," he offered, changing the subject and reaching for my hand while I reached for my napkin.

"Thanks. You too."

"How is your father?"

"Pretty good," I said. "Considering his age. Actually not that well. He has cancer."

"I'm sorry. He always had a strong will to live."

"That's one way to put it."

It went on like this, a polite volley of compliments and inquiries as the waiter arrived, then the salads, then the steaks.

"How's work?" he said.

"Great," I said. "I quit my job six months ago."

"What? You quit the plate factory?" We'd called it the plate factory. Some of his relatives, who agreed with my mother that Phillip was too handsome for me, thought I worked on an assembly line.

"Yup," I said, lifting a forkful of perfectly cooked flaky baked potato mounded with sour cream, butter and chives toward my mouth. This was the kind of place I'd eaten at as a child with my parents on Friday nights forty years ago, the kind of place they could get double martinis in big thick glasses with two olives apiece and kiddie cocktails for me and my sister, where you could still order surf and turf or Shrimp de Jonghe and baked Alaska for dessert. It was the kind of place where, when you arrived, they put a three-bowled stainless steel condiment dish on a lazy Susan in the middle of the table and you could ladle out corn relish, sweet pickles and small, brilliantly red, super-sweet candied apples to your heart's delight. No one I knew went to restaurants like this anymore and neither did I except with Phillip.

Being with Phillip made me feel decadent, unprincipled, unhinged from propriety. It always had. I wanted to eat everything and then smoke a cigar. Not only had I ordered a twelve-ounce rib eye steak, I'd asked for blue cheese dressing on my iceberg lettuce salad, extra sour cream for my potato and hollandaise sauce on my asparagus.

Phillip paused as he sliced his steak, waiting for an explanation. I patted my mouth with the huge linen napkin, leaving a pink lipstick stain, and took a sip of wine.

"Yes," I continued, squaring my shoulders. "It was time for a change. I'm actually working for a veterinarian now. I know," I said, noticing the slight lowering of his eyelids. "I know it's kind of an entrance level job. Doesn't pay much, but, you know how it goes," I was stalling, waiting for one of Donna's opaque slogans to come to mind. When it didn't I shrugged.

Fuck him, I thought. I buttered a warm Parker House roll. This was the last place on earth you could get the real thing, as far as I knew, and they were exactly what they should be, flaky and soft on the inside, with a perfectly smooth, browned cleft on top. They had to be homemade because no bakery still sold them. I'd looked everywhere. I intended to eat at least three.

I looked up. Phillip was still staring at me, holding his fork in the air.

"It started out as volunteer work but then he hired me, the vet I mean. I guess that's what happens," I said, remembering the phrase I'd been searching for. "When you follow your passion." I stuffed the buttered Parker House roll in my mouth. Heaven.

Phillip was nodding in a way that made it clear he disapproved, but the magic words had shut him up for a minute.

"So this job. This is what you plan to do?"

"Well, yes. But not only this." I paused to slice my steak. I took another sip of wine. It was liberating not to have to please him or even consider his opinion. I took my time.

"I've started a little business, actually. Consulting on funerals. I was going to tell you about it, you know, because of Sid."

Lying felt good. I drank more wine. It didn't matter how this turned out. He'd be leaving town next week. I could say anything, do anything. Throw wine in his face, go to bed with him.

Now he was looking a little confused. I wasn't the person he remembered leaving.

"I'm sorry about your dad," I added. "What happened finally?"

So Phillip, to avoid hearing any more about the new me, told me about his father's last illness, one of many, about his fourth and last wife, the one he'd married three months before he died, the controversy over the will, the medical bungling, the confusion over deeds to his various properties and, incredibly, his deathbed apology to Phillip for a lifetime of general bad behavior. Sid had grown up poor but died owning a chain of shoe stores, three condos, two Cadillacs, a broken-down racehorse named Shenanigans and a small plane he hadn't flown in sixteen years. There were three children by two wives and Phillip was the oldest, the only son.

"So how did you get into this, this line of work I mean?" He'd circled back to me.

For a split second I considered trying to explain about the women in the grocery store and how everything in my life seemed to be about death these days. But then I decided against it. "It just came naturally," I said. "I guess I'm just naturally mournful."

He nodded, not seeing the joke. "So can I hire you to help me? I'll pay whatever you're charging."

"Sure," I said, smiling at the waiter who was offering more wine. "I'll give you a deal. In memory of Vicious."

CHAPTER 38

K'uei / Opposition

Misunderstanding truth creates opposition.

Here's the thing. Saying goodbye to the beloved was difficult, the wasteland of emptiness afterward terrible. But the loving bereaved didn't need help planning the funeral. It was sad certainly, burdensome even, but they knew what to do; either it was prescribed to them through their religion or by a sense of what they had lost and how they wanted to honor it, him, her.

It was the ambivalent who needed help burying those to whom honor needed to be paid but for whom no one felt a clear uncomplicated love. Even Stan, who could have done it alone, needed help scattering his mother's ashes in a way that would accommodate his brother's mixed feelings. A service like mine was most useful to the seriously troubled. Phillip needed to bury Vicious, the shelter needed to put down Grace. These were not anyone's beloveds. There was no one to whom the task easily fell. Yet even the hard-hearted unforgiving knew that honor must be paid in death, even to the unlovable, particularly to the unlovable, I thought, who had received so little of it in life. The unloved life and its passing must be noted with gravitas, not in a personal way if that is not possible, but solemnly and without judgment, just to mark that it had come and gone. The fact of the life was infinitely more important than its particular quality or the affection it had aroused.

No third party would need to be called in when Bob died, I thought. Unless I died first. I would know what to do, be it brief or protracted, and it would be true. But for all the unloved there needed to be something, a moment of silence at least.

Phillip drove me home. He was planning to be in town a week, he said. He was flying back to Seattle the morning after the service; maybe we could get together again.

"I'm pretty busy," I said, ignoring his suggestion. "I'm working on another memorial now but I'll fit it in and email you. For old time's sake." He looked gloomy. I gave him a play punch in the shoulder as if we were old buddies but it only made him look worse. "Just send me what you have in mind and I'll take it from there."

I hoped Phillip didn't want to come in.

"And pick the music. You've got to have music." I remembered how Sid had turned the routine happy birthday song into an operatic exercise of his showy tenor. "If you send me something tomorrow, I'll try to get you an outline by the next day and then you can show it around and we'll take it from there."

"Don't you want to come over and see everybody? Linda would love to see you." He looked lost, his tan handsomeness out of place in the pale streetlight.

"I think this will work better," I said, giving him a peck on the cheek to signal that the evening was over. "Thanks for dinner." Then I ran to the house, where Clement was curled up on the front porch in an orange egg-shaped ball. I opened the door and he flowed in around my feet as I stepped inside, escorting me back to the bedroom. Bob was already in bed, his eyes half open, staring morosely into nothing as I undressed, threw my clothes over a chair and pulled on a big T-shirt. When I climbed into bed Clement hopped up and curled beside me, an award of affection he reserved for particularly difficult times. I lay bracketed by animals for a while, content. Then I heard Bob sigh and in my mind I heard him say "You may not still love him. But I do." I couldn't tell if was talking to me or to Clement.

CHAPTER 39

Chien / Obstruction

*Surrounded by obstructions, one must first retreat,
then seek the direction of the Sage.*

I woke up early the next morning and got right to work on Phillip's father's memorial. I had one day before Stan and I were scheduled to go through revisions on his mother's.

In the restaurant Phillip had said, "I guess I should ask you what you charge, but whatever it is, it's OK."

I'd given him a number, about what I would have charged for a week's worth of writing for my old boss. Phillip just nodded, chewing. "Next time charge more," he'd said, pointing his fork at me, a big chunk of pink meat still firmly speared on the end of it. "I'd pay double that."

Just to warm up I wrote a little remembrance of Sid, about his taking us to a White Sox game and singing "The Star-Spangled Banner" so dramatically that everyone in our section turned to watch and listen. He was the only one singing and might have been the only one in the stadium that day who knew all the words and could hit all the notes. He seemed happiest when he was singing for an audience, a syncopated version of "Happy Birthday" in a restaurant, a spontaneous syrupy rendition of "Some Enchanted Evening" while on line for a movie. Often when he finished, strangers applauded.

After I wrote the remembrance—maybe Phillip could read it, I thought, if he didn't want to write his own—I worked on the outline. First a psalm, then something from Phillip, then Linda's remembrance, if she'd be willing to say something, then their half-sister Judy. If any of them wanted to speak. My policy—already

I had one—was that survivors didn't have to. Central mourners, as I thought of them, might be too aggrieved but they also might be too angry or confused. Neighbors, old friends with selective memories, these were better. Beneficiaries of random kindness were best. Sid was a specialist in this, free Bears tickets to the neighbor down the hall, a surprise twenty-dollar bill inside a greeting card to someone else's troubled kid. I made a note to ask Phillip if he could come up with a list of people to call to see if they might speak.

As I worked, the memorial fell into shape and I thought it hardly seemed like something I could charge money for. It was too easy. But that was the point. It was only easy for me.

CHAPTER 40

Hsieh / Deliverance

A change in attitude delivers you from difficulties.

Stan called to say he'd found a home for Harvey. Family, three kids, one cat, a backyard. "They seem nice. So congratulations," he said. "He's your first graduate."

"What if he starts sniffing? Disease, I mean? Did you tell them about that trick?"

"No. Should I have?"

"What if he does it and they don't know what it is and they get mad at him for doing this thing I've been encouraging him to do and that might be really useful? It's a little intrusive unless you know. Shouldn't we tell them about his talent?"

Stan said probably but that I was on my own and gave me their phone number. I wrote it on a post-it note which I stuck to my computer and then promptly forgot about it along with the fourteen other post-it notes stuck there. They included the name of a new kind of therapeutic shoe that imitated the sensation of walking barefoot, a recipe for lemonade, a reminder to call my old friend Suzanne with the name of a book neither of us could remember when I'd last spoken to her a month ago, the word perseverant, the meaning of which I'd just learned, the date of my father's next doctor's appointment, the name of a new herbal food additive I thought might help Clement's breath, and a phone number I didn't recognize with a note that said "call him ASAP."

I heated up some lunch and went back to work on Phillip's father's service until, while eating a bowl of leftover potato soup at my desk (secret ingredients: rosemary, chicken broth and whipping cream), a post-it note fell into the soup. It was the phone number of the Kovaks, Harvey's new family.

I took it as a sign and dialed the number. I got Don, the father, and put him on speakerphone. I said I was the dog adoption placement coordinator and that I was doing an official well-being check on a recent placement and wanted to make sure everything was working out. Don told me about how much the kids already loved Harvey, how they'd renamed him Harry, how he'd eaten a Popsicle that made his tongue turn blue and how good he was with their cat. I said great and then I told him the story about Harvey sniffing my father and about the woman at the park.

"Hmmm, that's funny," he said. Then after a short silence, "He's been all over me in the strangest places. With his nose I mean."

"That's what I'm talking about," I said. "Maybe you should go to the doctor." It came out of my mouth without my being able to stop it. I knew better than to call up complete strangers and give them ominous news about their health but lately I had lost my capacity for politeness. It was as if some switch had been flipped and my ability to censor my own speech had been shut off. It seemed to have something to do with Phillip being so clearly out of my life. Not having to care what he thought about what I thought made everything so much easier. I hadn't realized it until he reappeared and suddenly I was grateful we'd had dinner together. Good old Phillip, the nicest thing about having seen him was knowing that soon I wouldn't have to. This must be the closure Donna talks about, I thought:

"I know. I've been meaning to make an appointment actually," Don was saying. "My wife keeps telling me about these disease sniffing dogs and I've got these, well, never mind. But you know. Who wants to go to the doctor."

"Well really you should," I said. "He's batting a thousand so far and I wouldn't risk it if I were you." I was becoming Donna.

Clement, who'd been listening the whole time, blinked slowly at Bob and then walked off. "No one is ready for death and yet it awaits us all," I could hear him say as he departed for the basement to contemplate the floor drain.

We ended the conversation with Don agreeing to make a doctor's appointment and saying he'd call me with the results. I said I'd be waiting to hear from him and that Harvey's favorite treat was corned beef hash from a can and that you could usually buy the house brand at Jewel on sale two-for-one. Don said he'd keep that in mind.

CHAPTER 41

Sun / Decrease

Be still, lessen the power of the ego,
and misfortune will be avoided.

After the ash-sprinkling ceremony by the river we all went to lunch at Sofia's Restaurant and Bar. I hadn't wanted to go. I hadn't felt it was appropriate for me to be there earlier either but Stan insisted after I told him about Phillip's father's funeral. He said I should, to see the results of my first project, since this was going to be a business.

"That's kind of awful," I said. "Like I'm some mercenary, funeral-crashing spy?"

"Then forget that. Just come with me. Please."

It went well. I'd written the service for comfort and contemplation, not for wrenching emotion out of the family. "Maryanne really goes for the gut," my old boss used to say approvingly in meetings when I'd turn in an especially smarmy verse. This was not meant to be that.

The remembrance part was the best. Everyone who knew Edith said something. Kay remembered how Edith swore at the food when she cooked and then emerged from the kitchen looking pleased and flushed, as if she'd won an argument. Julie, who'd driven in from Urbana the night before, remembered how her grandmother had made marshmallow sandwiches and let her share her bed when she stayed at her house on school vacations. Stan's brother Al remembered how his mother had fed the squirrels table scraps and raw eggs in the yard when he was a boy and how, after the neighbors complained, she continued to feed them on the sly, at night.

Stan seemed calm, relieved to have pulled it off, happy even in a subdued way. He had honored Edith by maintaining family harmony, something she would have approved.

"Do they know I'm the one who wrote it?" I'd whispered as we got out of his car in the restaurant parking lot, simultaneously brushing dog hair off our black clothes. I hoped not.

"No. I wasn't going to tell them, if you don't mind. They think I got it off the Internet. And they think you're my date." He took my hand.

"Date? Since when do you take a date to your mother's funeral?"

"You know what I mean."

I didn't actually, but I liked the feel of his warm, square, meaty, slightly hairy hand, roughened by years of caustic cleaning chemicals and the nipping of dogs and cats. I liked his muscular grip and his short clean fingernails, clipped straight across and so close that his square pink finger pads projected beneath them and pressed into my palm. I felt as trustful as one of his strays being led firmly to the examining table. I supposed I was one of his strays.

We ate at a Polish restaurant on Milwaukee Avenue that specialized in funeral lunches, a place with peeling wallpaper and tin ceilings. The service was family style, which meant they brought the food to the table in big oval bowls, with steam rising up as if in some cartoon enactment of plenty. Never mind that it was an unseasonably hot day in June with the air smelling of rotting peonies. The occasion called for long sleeves, black clothes and hot food. Here it was again. Death, life, food. The dead rested while the living ate. First there was a basket of freshly baked rye bread, then dishes of preserves, sour cream and soft sweet butter with spoons stuck in them, after that bowls of pale shiny sausage glistening with fat, then sauerkraut with caraway seeds in it, mashed potatoes, a platter of pierogies and a covered dish containing some dark stew I didn't recognize.

"Try the bigos," Kay said. "It's our only chance for vegetables."

Later she gave me her recipe for a simpler version of the same dish.

Everyone ordered drinks except for Julie who planned to make the three-hour drive back to school after lunch. Stan's aunt ordered a whiskey sour. Gene, her boyfriend, had an Old Style longneck, which he drank from the bottle. Edith's childhood friend Gert, who'd come in on the train from Milwaukee, drank a Manhattan and Kay downed a succession of martinis. Al and Stan drank Polish beer and I sipped an endless supply of sweet white wine from a small bowl-shaped glass that the waitress kept refilling from a cut-glass decanter.

After lunch and more drinks everyone hugged and got in their cars. Here is the recipe for bigos Kay wrote on the back of a Xeroxed poem in the parking lot after lunch. Hers is an Americanized version, she says. She makes it when someone has a death in the family, puts it in a casserole dish and then leaves it on their porch, along with brownies.

Kay's Bigos for Grief and Mourning

Quarter and cook 4 red potatoes, not too soft; then cut into thick slices with skins on.

Place in a large bowl.

Add 1 pound sauerkraut.

Halve ¼ pound of mushrooms and add.

Chop into slices 1 pound Polish sausage and add.

Quarter 2 yellow onions and add.

Add 1 large can stewed tomatoes.

Add 1 large can stewed plums.

Sprinkle with salt, pepper, garlic, caraway and dry mustard.

Fry ½ to 1 pound bacon in a large pan until it's crisp and crumbly.

Drain about half the fat, to taste, add the ingredients to the bacon and remaining fat and simmer until all is thoroughly cooked, at least ½ hour. If more liquid is needed, add beer. Stew on low for another hour.

Serve immediately or freeze.

The brownies, she says, she makes from a Duncan Hines mix.

I / Increase

Powerful improvements are underway.

When I woke up it was dark and still hot. Was it early morning and if so which one? Or was it the middle of the night? But then I realized someone else was in the bed and it wasn't Bob. Stan. There he was next to me, naked except for his wristwatch and a pair of tortoise-shell reading glasses, propped up on Bob's side of the bed, looking very brown and hairy against the white pillows. He seemed right at home as he stared at the sample AARP magazine I'd received the week before as a pre-fiftieth birthday promotional gift. Subscribe now, while there's still time before the big day and get half off. It was as good a way as any to tell your lover your age.

Stan had politely left the lamp off and was trying to read by streetlight. The room was hot, turgid. The air smelled sweetly of the dogwood tree outside the open window, plus sweat and another unmistakable aroma I hadn't smelled in a long time, all trapped in the thick summer air and going nowhere. Summer sex had a scent all its own.

Somehow it had become night. I glanced at the clock; it was almost nine. Bob needed a walk though he wasn't complaining yet. He was curled on his own bed in the corner of the room, a little glum and eyeing me discreetly with a sideways glance that I refused to meet. I was still slightly drunk and starting to feel hung over at the same time. I wondered absently how these two opposite sensations could coexist.

"Hi," I said.

"Greetings."

"It's OK if you need to go," I said. "I mean, aren't they all wondering where you are?"

"Probably not but I'll go pretty soon," he said, oblivious, or pretending to be, to the possibility that I was kicking him out, which I'd tried not to sound like I was doing. "We all need a little break from each other. Now that you're awake I think I will call the clinic, if you don't mind."

I closed my eyes. That wasn't so bad I thought, as he busied himself with the phone, not that I remembered much. I remembered the lunch, the wine, the parking lot embraces and promises to keep in touch. And had I accepted some drink called a Grasshopper? All that midday drinking in the heat was a mistake, no doubt, especially on top of the high emotion of the occasion. Still, it had made this possible.

After Phillip left I'd dreaded this, thinking it would be too strange and painful after all those years with him and then all those months without him. I'd been afraid any further attempt at a sexual life would be a pale pantomime of what it once had been. The cessation of sex with Phillip had been a death, the end of who I thought I was. I'd thought that part of my life was over, or that I should resolve that it was, as much as anything to avoid the shock of revisiting my body in this way, having to acknowledge how much I'd changed, inside and out. It had been a long time since I'd been seduced. Or seduced someone else, if that's what had happened. Though this wasn't seduction so much as—what? An agreement between friends. Had I finally, on the eve of my fiftieth birthday, become a consenting adult? Or did you have to be sober for that?

Why hadn't we done this sooner I thought, stealing a glance at Stan as I began to remember the events of the past few hours.

I picked up a magazine from my side of the bed and pretended to read too. I wondered if Stan had had as much to drink as I had. He didn't seem to be hung over. He was sitting up next to me now as if he spent every night of his life there, with the covers tucked neatly around his lap, pressing my phone against his ear as he listened to messages and nodded to himself. Somewhere he'd come up with paper and a pencil and was jotting notes.

"Buster's going to need surgery," he said, staring at my breasts as I got out of bed and wrapped myself in the kimono that was lying on the floor nearby.

I needed water. I stepped around a trail of discarded black clothes as I made my way to the kitchen. There on the counter was a tinfoil package of leftover bigos with a grease-stained Xeroxed poem on top with a recipe written in pencil on the back. Apparently we'd brought home food. There was cheesecake too, something I had no memory of, and it looked good.

"You hungry?" I called.

No answer. I heard the shower running and a few minutes later Stan appeared in the kitchen doorway with wet hair, wearing a towel. "Smells good," he said of the bigos, which I'd transferred to a bowl and placed in the microwave on a two-minute setting. Bob stood next to him, looking suspiciously damp, and smiling.

Overhead lights were out of the question, too hot and too harsh. I lit some candles and we sat down to dinner at the kitchen table, with Bob positioned contentedly on the floor between us.

CHAPTER 43

Kuai / Breakthrough (Resoluteness)

A breakthrough. Do not be drawn back into bad habits.

A week later the heat wave had still not broken but since neither Stan nor I minded I hadn't turned the air conditioning on yet. We had all the windows and doors open, the fans on and the lights off and were eating dinner in the dark with candles at the kitchen table again as we had every night since Edith's memorial. Stan had made a salad with boiled eggs, potatoes, sardines and olives on top and I had put out some crackers and sliced lemons. Stan was explaining how the ticks were bad this year and said he was recommending Lyme disease vaccinations for all dogs when Bob ran barking and wagging to the back door.

I heard a familiar voice coming through the screen, "Hey Bobbo, anybody else home?" It was Phillip, standing on the porch behind the screen door. He was holding a cold bottle of white wine. I could see the silvery beads of condensation on its neck when he moved into the light. Stan, who was wearing a pair of orange gym shorts and nothing else, had just speared half a boiled egg with a fork and was preparing to raise it to his mouth. There were crumbs in his beard and down the front of my open kimono. I brushed the crumbs off my breasts, tied the kimono closed and walked to the door.

"Hi." I said. "We're just having dinner. You want to come in? This is Stan. Stan, this is Phillip. My ex."

Stan put down his fork and stood up so they could shake hands. Stan was half a foot shorter than Phillip in his bare feet, which had the same clean square frankness of his hands but were smoother, unmangled by dog bites, and therefore looked soft and childlike. He was glowing with sweat—the house really did get hot—and patches of curly hair stood up on his shoulders like epaulets. Phillip, in contrast, was smooth and cool as always. He hated heat but he showed no signs of suffering from it. No doubt he'd had the air conditioning on high in his rental car. He looked particularly cool in comparison to Stan, tall and elegant in the neatly pressed shirt that brought out the blue in his eyes.

"Nice to meet you, Phil," Stan offered.

"Lip," Phillip said.

"Excuse me?"

"Phillip," I said apologetically to Stan. "He goes by Phillip."

"Ah. Nice to meet you, Phillip."

Stan sat down and resumed eating. Phillip stood inside the door and said he'd stopped by to report that he was leaving town tomorrow and wanted to thank me again for planning the service. It had gone well.

"It's too bad you couldn't make it," he said, glancing sideways at Stan, as if he suspected it was his fault. Clement had arrived from the basement and was now silently winding figure eights around Phillip's ankles. Phillip knelt to scratch him and Clement purred.

"How's my kitcatboy?" he said to Clement in an intimate voice.

"I think it was better I wasn't there," I said. "But I'm glad it went well."

"Thanks to you," he said in a burst of morose chivalry, standing up. Now he was acting the part of the wronged husband, visiting the animal children and scanning the kitchen possessively, while sneaking glances at Stan. It was his kitchen too, or it had been. I had taken his mementos, affixed with magnets, off the refrigerator, thrown out his special condiments, drunk his beer. Suddenly I saw the room through his eyes—denuded of him though he'd built the cabinets, fixed the faucet, cooked thousands of meals at the stove. Now Stan's grubby briefcase, bulging with files and smelling faintly of disinfectant and dog dander, was sitting on the counter next to the stainless steel bread box that he, Phillip, had bought at considerable expense online from a Swedish kitchen supply store.

Did he feel ownership, nostalgia or only territorial envy for Stan who was sitting in his place at the table? Did he regret leaving or only regret that he hadn't called before coming over? Stan, his posture very straight, was quietly munching his egg.

For a moment I thought I might invite Phillip to join us at the table but the fact that Stan was wearing so little, and that I was, made it awkward, suggested recent sex. It hadn't been the evening Phillip had planned, I could tell. The wine hinted at more tender intentions than this cursory visit.

"Now that you're here, do you want to take anything?" I said. It was an awkwardly timed offer but I wished he would. "What about all that stuff of your grandfather's in the basement—couldn't you use it in your new place?"

"I have to tell you though," I said in a lower voice, "I did throw out some stuff, sorry." I had led him away from Stan, into the dining room where the table we had bought together at a flea market years before was piled with research material on funerals. Already I was working on another memorial service for someone Donna had recommended when she got wind of what I'd been up to.

"You threw my stuff out?" Phillip looked up from the pages of the *Mourners' Kaddish* he'd been riffling. His posture stiffened as a little of the old fury flashed.

"What was I supposed to do with it?" I could hear my voice rising, becoming defensive. I didn't want to fight in front of Stan. "This isn't really a very good time but you could, you know, come back with a truck and take what's yours—maybe tomorrow? That bookcase in the basement was your grandfather's. You should take it."

He exhaled dramatically and looked sourly around shaking his head no. He'd already said he was flying out tomorrow. His skin suddenly looked very pink but his hair was still neat. I touched his shoulder, I wanted to console him. He seemed so pathetic, probably on purpose. I wondered if he'd found someone to settle down with or if he'd already moved on. I supposed that right now he was feeling sorry he'd left, or sorry he'd left the house and the animals, sorry there was someone sleeping in what used to be his bed and eating at what used to be his table. His sorry-ness made me feel sorry for him and I hoped what he was going back to made him happy. But I wanted to finish my dinner. I wanted him gone.

"I'll come back with a truck, sometime, in a month or two," he said picking up a candlestick that had been a gift from his mother, his other hand buried in the fur around Bob's neck. Bob was wagging furiously, looking up at Phillip now with his mouth half open and his forehead deeply furrowed in a look of anxious supplication. "A lot of this stuff is mine you know."

"I know it is. I just wish you'd take it."

He planted a proprietary kiss on my cheek, tucked the candlestick under his arm and waved to Stan, grabbing the wine bottle as he left. The screen door banged shut behind him.

"I'll fix that spring tomorrow," Stan said and then called "Come here, boy," to Bob who stood in the middle of the kitchen staring out the back door still wagging his tail, but tentatively. He looked confused at first and then trotted over to Stan, who fed him a whole sardine.

CHAPTER 44

Kou / Coming to Meet

Darkness reappears unexpectedly.
Caution and reticence are in order.

I had planned to introduce my father to Stan the following Sunday. I warned him the food would be soft and bland. He said that was fine with him. I got up early Sunday morning to go to the grocery store and by nine o'clock I had made a tuna casserole with potato chips and melted cheese on top. I was planning to serve an ice cream cake roll for dessert. Stan had agreed to show up during the cheese and martini course—he was bringing a green bean casserole he promised to leave the almonds out of so that it would be soft—but my father called around ten to say he didn't feel up to going out. I offered to bring the tuna casserole over to him but he said no, he thought he'd just rest. I called Stan and told him he was off the hook and he said he'd been looking forward to it and asked if I shouldn't go over anyway to check up on him. He offered to come along and bring his casserole and his medical bag. I said thanks but I'd go alone. I called my father back and told him I was coming over to drop off some food.

When I got to his house no one answered the door so I let myself in with my bent skeleton key. Despite the early blooming dogwoods and the still-searing June heat the house was cool and dark and smelled stale, a blend of dirty blankets and boiled cabbage, with undertones of Sloan's liniment, bacon grease, overripe bananas and sweet rotting roses one of the women from his church had brought the week before.

My father was dozing in his kitchen chair next to the stove, his head on his chest, with the oven on and open, the temperature turned up to three hundred degrees. He seemed to have telescoped down inside his clothes; he was wearing the same long underwear and flannel shirt he wore every day, plus mittens and a scarf. He hadn't shaved in days and white stubble stood out on his bluish skin, a sight I'd rarely seen. The sound of me setting down heavy dishes woke him up.

"I can't get warm," he said rising shakily to greet me, explaining the oven situation. He looked like a small, pale child dressed in a woodsman costume, swaddled inside layers of oversized plaid clothes, clothes that had once fit him, snugly even. I settled him back at the table and set the tuna casserole down on the stove. I realized I'd packed it in a big ceramic dish with a glass top that, full, was too heavy for him to lift. In my kitchen it had looked generous and festive but here it just looked huge and gross, enough food, as he might have said, to choke a horse.

"You want a little casserole now? It's still warm," I said and then to make it seem less daunting, "I'm going to put this into smaller bowls for you."

"Maybe later. Why don't you take some home?" I could tell he didn't like the looks of it. He was gesturing weakly toward the refrigerator with his cane as if to ward off unwanted food and as he did I could see the concave waistband of his pants, how the cloth hung from him like a curtain.

It had been less than a week since I'd seen him but he'd lost more weight.

"Dad, are you eating?"

"I'm drinking Hawaiian Punch," he said, evasively. "I love that Hawaiian Punch." His doctor had assigned him to drink three bottles of calorie-packed nutrition supplement every day, but he poured it down the sink and left the empty cans in the trash to fool me. He preferred Hawaiian Punch spiked with a little gin.

"How about eating just a little?"

He shook his head. "It just doesn't appeal," he said, looking vaguely surprised. He didn't know what to make of it either. He'd always had a hearty appetite. It had been a point of pride for him that he ate robustly, excessively even, and never got fat, encouraging me to do the same. When I was a child, when my mother didn't feel like getting out of bed, he'd cooked the Sunday roasts he remembered from his own childhood. He'd put the meat and potatoes in the oven in his mother's cast-iron pot before he left for church and then come home and make gravy and boil vegetables with a touch of baking soda, to keep the color he said. When he retired he took over all the cooking, branching out into fruit pies and cornbread. My mother had ceded the territory without protest or even a comment.

He sipped the pink liquid through an elbow straw stuck in a juice glass. "I love this stuff," he said.

"Why don't you lie on the couch. While I put the food away."

He slowly made his way to the living room. I settled him under a frayed blanket and then went back to the kitchen to divide up the casserole into plastic freezer dishes left from various neighbors' donations. They were always dropping off food and formerly he'd eaten it with savor and then written enthusiastic, descriptive thank you notes in the form of haiku about how much he'd enjoyed it, returning the dishes with the notes inside.

But apparently he hadn't returned any plastic containers lately and they were piling up on his counter top. One contained a scrap of paper on which he'd written: "Your salubrious / Casserole warms my gizzard / Brightens up my day." Another held the message: "Butter cookies with / Gin at bedtime convey me / To the land of nod."

His refrigerator held more plastic containers, these full of unidentifiable food of indeterminate age from the same well-meaning neighbors. Who knew how long it had been there. I wondered if I dared throw some of it out. If he noticed he'd be furious.

After I'd put all the food away—I'd brought the ice cream cake roll too and the cheeses I'd planned to serve as appetizers and some fresh bananas, though the ones I'd brought four days before were still uneaten—I went to check up on him. He was sound asleep.

CHAPTER 45

Ts'ui / Gathering Together

To lead others toward the good,
one must purify one's own character.

The false bright summer of early June became the real summer of July, a month of oppressive heat, gray white skies and unrelenting humidity, weeks on end of eighty nine-degree nights, ninety four-degree days when the sky ached to rain and instead just leaked. The air hung still and heavy, full of every cooking and toilet smell from the past month, now all mixed together and gone rancid. Nature's ventilation system had been shut off and the only alternative was even worse, the stale metallic chill of air conditioning. Even the flowers smelled bad. The lilacs and peonies that had made the June mornings so sweet had given way to brighter, sturdier garden flowers reeking of pollen and heavy perfume—tough roses trained to grow over unsightly garages, paint box zinnias and turpentine-smelling marigolds lining already overgrown vegetable gardens. The night air buzzed with crickets and mosquitoes that flew through torn screens and stung us as we tried to sleep on damp sheets when we dared to leave the windows open. June bugs, that arrived a month late every year, propelled themselves like hulking tanks with failing engines through my kitchen at night, feasting on fallen Cheerios and left-out dog food. They were slow and stupid, easy to catch, failing to understand the danger they courted, trusting that Bob wouldn't eat them, that Clement wouldn't torture them, that I wouldn't crush them under my shoe, too dim to conceive that I might, too dim to conceive that I even existed. But their imbecility made me merciful and instead I trapped them under drinking glasses, slid cardboard junk mail ads underneath to contain them and carried them outside. Let some other creature kill and eat them.

Bob suffered in the heat, even with air conditioning, refusing food as he lay on his side and panted shallowly. When I did turn the air on I did it for him. The heat made me think of his age and his graying coat; he would be eight years old soon.

But Clement thrived, jungle beast that he was. He no longer left his pristine gifts for me on the porch. I didn't know what signaled the change, maybe the turn of seasons or maybe Stan's arrival in our lives, taking on the role of newcomer and provider. Whatever it was, Clement now appeared to have decided he was a full-fledged member of the household and no longer needed to pay his dues. He was hunting more than ever from the looks of things and now in place of his carefully arranged offerings, circumspectly left intact, I sometimes found remains of rabbits in the yard when I went to pick up sticks after it rained.

But if the time for his gifts had passed his reticence had too. We had become a kind of family and Clement had gone from being a charming but mysterious guest to a full brother. He liked to sit on the kitchen table and watch me cook, inclining his head attentively as I moved about. Sometimes he made little chirping sounds, small wows that slowly became louder when I took certain foods from the refrigerator. Then he paced up and down the counter, as if on patrol, and bumped my hand with his head to make me spill. He liked to drink milk from a glass and when I carried him from room to room in my arms he reclined trustfully and patted my cheek with his paw.

He revealed himself to be surprisingly social. He'd always liked my father, when he was still able to visit, and now he waited at the front door for the mailman's daily visits, trotting out to greet him at the curb and then escorting him back to the house.

And best of all he seemed to like Bob. On idle afternoons they'd lie curled back to back in bed, dozing. Sometimes when I entered a room I'd find them staring at each other, apparently in deep conversation, but when I tried to join in, they played dumb and all I got was static. Then, feeling left out, I'd scoop up Clement in my arms and dangle him upside down to touch noses with Bob and we'd all pretend for a while they were only cute pets.

CHAPTER 46

Shêng / Pushing Upward

*Activity grounded in truth
brings progress and good fortune.*

Stan wanted to take a vacation and he wanted me to come along. It was August, slow season at the clinic, and the month when he usually took time off. Last summer he'd taken Julie on a five-day cruise up the Alaskan coast as a graduation present. We could do that, he said, but a longer one that went farther. Too expensive I said. I'll pay he said. No I said. Africa? He countered. He had a friend at a wildlife refuge in Kenya. I would love it he said. Even more expensive I said. He said his friend would put us up. All we had to do was get there. Still too much I said.

"Ah," Stan said. That meant he understood. I couldn't leave my father now. But I couldn't say it because when I talked about it people told me not to get sucked in, sucked down and I was tired of hearing it. How did you not? They were the same people who arranged for other people to get sucked in so they wouldn't have to.

"What if we just went camping for a few days," Stan said. "Michigan. Eight hours will get us to the Upper Peninsula. Six-and-a-half hours and a speeding ticket will get us back. If necessary. We can take the dogs."

"Good idea," said Bob, who had been lying quietly on the floor beside the bed during this conversation, looking worried. The possibility of his inclusion cheered him right up. Now he looked at me. "Let's do it," he said so loudly I couldn't believe I was the only one who heard.

I tried to ignore him but I couldn't think of a reasonable objection. I remembered liking camping, a long time ago, before Phillip. I hadn't done it in decades or not successfully at least. Phillip wouldn't consider it. Why would we leave our perfectly nice home to go somewhere without running water he argued and it was hard to argue back. He preferred cities and good hotels near excellent restaurants or at least resorts with clean beaches, heated pools and well-stocked bars. Not that I'd minded. Camping was a romantic notion, as much as anything, one, which, if you didn't share it, just seemed bizarre. Instead we'd gone to London, Montreal, Prague, Paris, San Francisco, places where we could eat well and where there were enough distractions to cover up our silences. You could get along with almost anyone in Paris; to share a tent you had to really like them. I couldn't complain, though Phillip's refusal to try camping even once bothered me. For one thing it made it impossible to travel with Bob, dear Bob who hated to be left behind.

Once I'd bought a cheap pup tent and driven Bob to a state park in Wisconsin by myself, when Phillip was off on some business trip, but it wasn't any fun and I came back early. What would have been peaceful and meditative with two was disconcertingly lonely alone. Sitting next to a campfire cooking a meal for myself and Bob while reading a newspaper in the dimming light seemed conspicuously odd and antisocial, an absurd, pointless hardship, rather than the adventurous getaway I had remembered from my college days, the beginning of a decline into some kind of madness. Even Bob didn't seem to enjoy it, refusing at first to even get out of the car. As it grew dark I worried he'd bolt and be attacked by bears or shot by another camper who thought he was one. He was glum and as out of his element as I was, lying by the fire and refusing to eat his bratwurst. Finally in the middle of the night he poked a hole in the cheap tent and walked through it, disappearing for what seemed like hours. Later he reappeared and curled up beside me and soon fell fast asleep while I, with his leash now firmly clipped to his collar and wound around my wrist, lay awake for the rest of the night.

As soon as it got light we left, only stopping once on our way back at a McDonald's where I bought us each a fish sandwich and a bottle of water. I never told Phillip about the trip and never knew if he'd tried to call that night.

This though might be fun. Stan wanted to bring his canoe—the dogs love it, he said—and spend ten days, but that was too long. Too long to be alone together and too long away from my father.

There were signs. He hadn't been to my house in weeks. Now I went to his house three or four times a week to bring food he wouldn't eat. Stan had started to come along on these visits, with his vet bag in the car, just in case. My father didn't ask about Stan's presence on these visits, just happily accepted when he offered to take out the garbage or change a light bulb. My father's natural curiosity had disappeared. Other people didn't interest him anymore. He was shedding the personal, returning to a kind of generalized self that was all about his body, his needs. Sometimes we brought along Bob and Bathsheba, the calmest of Stan's dogs, and they climbed up beside him on the couch or lay at his feet, companionably nibbling crumbs they found in his pant cuffs.

The night after Stan suggested a camping trip, Donna stopped by with leftovers from some fundraiser she was on her way home from—one third of a chocolate sheet cake, a bucket of fried chicken and a half-eaten tub of coleslaw. She knew I was taking food to my father these days and suggested I take it to him.

"Thanks, but not this time," I said, thinking the food would more than last him the rest of his natural life. I told her how, the last time I'd been there, he'd slept for most of my visit and eaten a total of four M&Ms. I told her how he'd lost his house key and how I'd spent an hour looking for it and found it under the toilet. I told her he seemed to have daily problems now, daily losses. I told her Stan wanted to take a vacation.

"Go," she said. "I can check up on your dad. Not a problem." She had gotten to know him over the years, stopping in on our Sunday dinners, more often after Phillip was gone. She'd even brought Felicia a few times, and after opening his eyes wide the first time I introduced Felicia as Donna's partner, he seemed to take it in stride. He liked Donna. She listened to his stories and brought him food. He'd even written her a poem about her vegan chili, which ended with the line "I love it, really!"

"Really?" I said.

"Really. I like the guy. I'd be happy to keep an eye on him."

"It's too much to ask."

"Yeah but you didn't ask. I offered."

"Let me think about it."

CHAPTER 47

K'un / Oppression (Exhaustion)

An unavoidable time of adversity.
Quiet strength insures a later success.

So we planned a one-week trip to Porcupine Mountain Wilderness State Park in the Upper Peninsula of Michigan. This was our compromise. If something happened and we needed to get back, we could be home in seven hours. Donna had Stan's cell phone number and Stan would keep his phone on so that he could keep in daily touch with the clinic. The plan was that Donna would call my father every day and stop over every other day with food. There was a pizza recipe she wanted to try out on him, she said, swore it would bring his appetite back. She would also check in on Clement and make sure he was in or out as he preferred and that his food bowl was always full. Of course, she said, she would also pet him.

Stan made reservations for a rustic waterfront campsite in a virgin hardwood hemlock forest on the shores of Lake Superior and over the next week we started to assemble supplies on my dining room table. The pile grew: a camp stove, a cooler, Stan's dome tent, a kerosene lantern, two large bags of trail mix, a flashlight, fleece blankets. We each contributed what we had or what we were moved to buy so it soon became a disorderly and eclectic mix reflecting our different visions of what camping was or might be. On his daily visits Stan added to the pile two down sleeping bags, an axe, a box of kitchen matches, two containers of Wet Wipes, a first aid kit, a battered frying pan, air mattresses for us and the dogs. "They'll hog ours," he'd said knowingly. "They need their own."

"You've done this before," I said.

"Yep," he said.

Among my contributions were candles, bug spray, picnic-sized salt and pepper shakers, toilet paper, a case of red wine, a spatula, a cork screw, graham crackers, marshmallows, Hershey bars, binoculars, miniature bottles of balsamic vinegar and olive oil, a head of garlic, cracked coffee cups, paper plates, a stack of library books, a bird whistle, a forty-pound bag of dog food and more toilet paper.

Stan and all his dogs slept over the night before we left so we could get an early start. The dogs were fine on the drive up though they filled Stan's Subaru station wagon with a wet musky odor that made us keep the windows open. They were a collection of sweet mixed breed castoffs with various treatable ailments who'd been brought to him to be killed. He had refused and adopted them. There were three, Elliott, Roy and Bathsheba; Roy was a small Corgi mix and shared the front seat with us. The other two and Bob, who were all about the same size and good friends by now, slid and bumped around on the back seat, jostling for access to the open windows.

The trip got easier as we got farther from the city. The dogs calmed down and as the outside air smelled better, so did the inside air and by the time we crossed the Wisconsin border all three dogs in back were dozing in a pile.

"Time for breakfast," Stan said somewhere after Waukesha. The deal we'd struck was that we'd eat bananas in the car and have a real breakfast on the road to escape rush hour and cover some ground early. We began to search for a suitable diner and found one twenty miles up the highway. "The Ham 'n' Egger" said the pink neon sign. "Breakfast 24 Hours a Day." Trucks filled the parking lot, and the place reeked of grease.

It looked promising; we pulled in.

After fried eggs, breakfast sausage, buttered toast, hash browns, fruit salad, pancakes and two extra orders of sausage wrapped in napkins for the dogs, we were back on the road.

A companionable silence settled over our little traveling party. We had reached a new level of comfortable togetherness. I liked it that Stan didn't feel the need to fill the air with conversation, and finally it was me who broke the silence.

"Does it ever bother you that life doesn't seem to have a plot?" It was the first time I'd spoken to him of my ongoing preoccupation with this subject. We'd never been together this long with nothing else to do. I said this as we hurtled past a picturesque clump of Holstein cows, the living embodiment of plotlessness, all standing next to a pond, mottled by the sun and shade and facing north.

Stan's eyebrows shot up and his neatly trimmed beard quivered a little but he just kept driving. My problem, Phillip had told me many times, was that I didn't know how to conduct polite conversation. I went from morose silence to weird obsessive ponderings without ever mentioning the weather. It was creepy and embarrassing at parties, he said, and it made him nervous. Now I was at it again. Car trips were the test of a relationship.

Stan kept driving. I couldn't tell if his continued silence was contemplative—was he considering his answer?—or stonewalling. Was he refusing to answer, not stooping to partake in the negativity of such a thought? Or maybe he was mulling it over and his silence was an invitation to keep talking.

"I mean it seems like nothing happens in any particular order that has meaning. Not that that's bad, it's just different from what you're taught or what I thought, that life has this narrative order that proceeds in a certain meaningful way from birth to death. But what if it doesn't? Like the fact that we're driving to Michigan right now. It's nice and in one sense it seems inevitable but in another it just seems, I don't know. Random. Like it doesn't matter if we do it or not."

I looked down at my lap to see Roy staring at me as if he was listening and waiting for a conclusion, a consensus to be arrived at and announced by the two controlling beings in the car. His big Corgi ears were sticking straight out on either side of his head, like wings on an ill-designed and impossibly fat craft that could never fly. I rubbed his belly and he closed his eyes, his pale eyelashes fanning out peacefully on the carmel-ly brown fur of his face.

"Not that I have a problem with that," I continued. "I like it. In fact I am very happy right now, happy to be outside of history. You know? Like, it doesn't matter whether we're here or not. That's a very pleasant feeling to me, a relief. People always complain when they look at the stars and feel insignificant but I just feel relieved. That's another reason I like camping. The stars, I mean. That and the food," I added, trying to bring it back to something easy.

It really was time to stop talking, but Stan's silence was like an empty bowl to pour my thoughts into. When he still didn't say anything I said, "Do you ever feel that way? Do you ever wish something would happen?"

Still nothing. I looked over at him. "Or is the plot just that we roam around waiting for something to happen until we die, and that's the thing we were waiting for? Or do you just wish I would stop talking?"

More silence. Then, finally, slowly, with the studied patience of someone who no longer feels patient but wishes to appear so, he said, "No I don't wish you'd stop talking. I'm just thinking. I'm thinking that things do happen, Maryanne. All the time. You'd notice they're always happening if you paid attention. The dogs are happening. We're happening."

I couldn't tell if he sounded angry, annoyed or just nonplussed. Roy, who had rolled his thick body slowly onto his other side, like a self-turning roast, had burrowed his spine into my body by now; his eyes squinted shut. He yawned and wagged his broad stub of a tail once or twice and then relaxed even more deeply into my lap. He seemed to like the vibrations in my body when I spoke. One of my hands rested on his chest, which moved up and down evenly, like a furry bellows.

"Are you annoyed or just nonplussed?" I asked.

"I'm not annoyed," he said, definitely sounding annoyed this time. "I just disagree. I think there is a plot, as you call it. I think the plot is you try to live your life well, and not be an asshole.

That's already a lot. You try to take care of yourself and the other beings in your world, and help things live in as minimally painful a way as possible and lots of things fight you along the way and then yes eventually you die and these other creatures you try to defend, people, animals, whatever, die too but the fight goes on."

Stan had sped up and was passing a convoy of semis. He must have been doing eighty. "In the meantime plenty of things happen," he continued, glancing into his rearview mirror at the truck driver who was giving him the finger. "Lots of things, Maryanne, some crucial and some trivial but all in all almost more things than you can stand to have happen if you're paying attention. Haven't you noticed that enough things have happened to you already? I think that is the plot, Maryanne. Isn't that enough? What's wrong with that?"

I'd never heard him make such a long speech.

"Nothing," I said. "Nothing's wrong with it. Actually, I like that version of things. I like it a lot."

CHAPTER 48

Ching / The Well

Return to the well of goodness.

I'd gone foraging for dry wood as soon as we arrived, while Stan pitched the tent. When we were ready to cook dinner we lit the fire and continued to stoke it as the night grew dark. Now it was late and we were letting it burn out.

We'd made dinner from supplies we'd picked up at a little camp store on our way in. In addition to food and ice, we'd bought lottery tickets and, on impulse, three six-dollar green plaid flannel shirts, one large, two small. One of the small ones was to be a souvenir for my father.

We were well into our second bottle of red wine as the fire died down. Elliot, Roy and Bathsheba were lounging in the dirt, staying close to us and to what was left of the food while Bob, perhaps remembering his earlier aborted camping trip, had let himself into the tent and gone to bed. I was toasting marshmallows on a green stick.

"So you find all these stars, all these possible other worlds, reassuring," Stan said, revisiting our earlier conversation as he poured himself more wine.

"Well," I said. "It does take the pressure off us to lead meaningful lives." When he didn't answer I said, "How about you?"

He was lying on his back on a log but managed to shrug. There were bits of leaves stuck in his hair and beard. "I don't think about it very much," he said, sitting up to poke the fire with a long stick. "Seems like there's enough else to worry about here. Or to enjoy, for that matter. I mean, if there are people out there in other galaxies, good for them. Our lives are what matter to us. Or should."

I was wrapped in a fleece blanket, sitting next to the fire, but I felt a chill. His careful construction, "should," suggested a not-so subtle judgment. I needed to defend myself, I thought, at least to say I didn't mean I didn't care about him.

"I don't mean I don't care about you. Or us. I just sometimes worry that none of it matters."

He didn't say anything for a long time and then he resumed poking the logs, separating them so they would burn out safely and we could go to bed. They collapsed into little constellations of sparks and then went suddenly dark. It was his way of announcing the evening was over.

Finally he said, "You just have to decide that it matters, Maryanne. You just have to pick something and care about it. I don't give a shit what you pick. It doesn't have to be me. Just pick something. Don't you know that? Otherwise how the fuck are you going to live the rest of your life?"

Now I'd done it. When we got into our sleeping bags he kept his zipped.

Fried Camping Potatoes for Comfort
in Case of Emotional Distance

Scrub and thinly slice 4 redskin potatoes.

Fry ½ pound bacon until crisp on cast-iron campground grill over open fire.

While bacon fries, add potatoes.

Later as potatoes soften add 1 large sliced onion.

Add 1 sliced green pepper.

Crumble crisp bacon into mixture as it cooks.

Season with salt and pepper.

(This is better if you boil the potatoes first.)

CHAPTER 49

Ko / Revolution

Devotion to truth enables a revolution.

Stan's cell phone rang inside the pocket of his new green flannel shirt early the next morning while we were finishing breakfast. The shirt was balled up on the picnic table under a pile of paper plates, which was weighted down with an illustrated guide to the birds of North America. We'd cooked the rest of the bacon and then fried eggs and bread and the leftover potatoes from the night before in the bacon grease, filling up the woods around us with the sweet smoky smell of cooked fat and driving the dogs crazy.

Stan was in the tent digging around for paper towels when the first bars of a Bach fugue rose muffled and distorted out of the mess on the picnic table. It took me a minute to realize it was the phone. When I did, I hesitated before I picked it up. It was Donna calling from the hospital to say she'd stopped at my father's house that morning and found him disoriented, in pain, angry when she tried to coax him into the car so she could drive him to the ER. Finally, when she couldn't wrangle him into the car by herself, she'd called an ambulance and was now at the hospital waiting while they examined him.

"I'm so sorry, Stan," I said, as soon as I'd hung up. "I have to go back."

He nodded. He'd heard my half of the conversation and was already pulling damp sleeping bags and pillows out of the tent. "We can make it in seven hours if we haul," he said. "Don't need to stop except to gas up."

We had the tent down and the car packed and the dogs exercised and loaded up in less than an hour.

We headed out in a different kind of silence than the one in which we'd begun.

"I don't feel so good," I said after a few miles.

"Yeah," he said.

We drove almost two hundred miles without saying another word, except to the dogs and to Donna who called three more times to say there was no news, until I had to ask Stan to stop at a gas station.

"I really appreciate this," I said as I got out of the car stiffly and as he gathered up the four leashes in an attempt to save time by walking all the dogs at once.

"When you gotta go you gotta go," he said.

"You know what I mean," I said. "I mean your coming all this way and then just turning around and going back. I appreciate it."

"It's just what you do, Maryanne. No need to thank me." Apparently he was still annoyed. I didn't press it.

Stan drove the whole way home, directly to the hospital, and dropped me off in the street in front of the long wall of plate glass windows at the front entrance. He said he was going to head back to his house to let the dogs out and unload the car.

"I'll take Bob home with me," he said. "Just in case."

"In case of what?"

"In case you need to stay."

I wasn't ready. My clothes smelled like smoke and bacon. I'd had too much red wine to drink the night before, I was stiff from sitting in a car for seven hours and from having spent the night in a tent, on the floor, having been shoved off the air mattress in my sleep by the collective weight of four dogs. I'd been eating greasy food for two days and, with an uneasy mind and four dogs scratching and moaning in their sleep and bumping each other and me out of place all night inside a hot tent next to a pissed-off boyfriend who refused to have sex, I hadn't slept much. I needed a nap. Also a hot bath, a cup of tea, a bowl of fruit salad and clean clothes. And some time alone to think. I wondered irrelevantly how Clement was and suddenly I wanted nothing more than to lie down with him somewhere in a clean manless dogless place and stroke his beautiful orange fur.

"Are you going to be alright?" Stan said, in a tone suggesting just how un-alright I looked. "I need to get these guys home but I can come back and stay with you for awhile. If you want."

"No, thanks. It's OK," I said, "I'm OK." What I meant was that I was working toward numb and that it would be easier to remain in that condition if he weren't around.

A horn sounded behind us. "I have to move. Call me," Stan said reaching through the window and squeezing my arm. I stood on the curb a minute longer, postponing the inevitable, and watched as Stan's car pulled away, dog heads sticking out of every window. I waved weakly looking at my own hand, thinking I needed to clean my fingernails.

CHAPTER 50

Ting / The Cauldron

*You serve as an example to others by sacrificing your ego
and accepting the guidance of the Higher Power.*

I sat in an orange plastic chair in room 946B. We were on the ninth floor. Nine B meant oncology. Despite the late summer's long-lasting light, the room was dark, cast into permanent twilight by heavy curtains, and it smelled of chicken broth, talcum powder and disinfectant. A Foley bag full of bloody urine hung on the side of the bed. A small form lay flat and still under the sheets, taking up so little space it was hard to tell someone was there: the form was my father. Nurses and aides in pastel scrubs with exotic-sounding names came and went, checking his pulse and blood pressure and jiggling the IV tubes that hung from his body. Their visits were oddly comforting. We exchanged pleasantries, small jokes. Someone wearing pink with a nametag that said Vandana Shiva flipped up a panel on the end of the bed to reveal blinking red lights. When she punched a button my father's weight lit up in pounds: 102.

"Ha ha, I'm glad my bed doesn't do that," said Vandana Shiva as she wrote the number down in my father's chart.

I asked her if my father's doctor would be by any time soon.

"No. He is gone for the day," she said. "Tomorrow maybe."

A thick curtain hung across the middle of the room dividing my father's side from his roommate's. Another very old man, named Mr. Krebbs, was in the next bed. I knew his name because every time a nurse went to check on him she addressed him formally.

Mr. Krebbs moaned rhythmically. When the orderly brought him a tray of food, the curtain opened and I could see Mrs. Krebbs sitting next to him in an orange chair identical to mine, stroking his blue hand. Ever since I'd arrived she'd been there, talking to him—she called him Norm—and muttering gossip about people they knew while he moaned. She ate his dinner and told him what it tasted like. Sometimes she cried.

When I'd first arrived my father was conscious enough to complain loudly about Mr. Krebbs' moaning. I could tell he hoped that Mr. Krebbs would overhear him and stop. When that didn't work he called out for Mr. Krebbs to shut up. Soon after that a nurse came in and gave my father a shot. Now he was sound asleep and had been for what seemed like a long time. I had lost all sense of time and there was no clock in the room. I had purposely taken my watch off for camping and never put it back on. I didn't even know where it was, folded up in the tent maybe.

I wanted to get out of the orange chair. I hobbled to the nurses' station—sitting so long on plastic had made me even stiffer—and saw that it was after nine o'clock. I'd been there over four hours; I must have slept. I went into the family lounge where Melea, the last shift's nurse, had already shown me how to use the VCR. There was a collection of Disney movies I could watch and she invited me to help myself to bottled water, coffee, cookies. I should feel at home she said. The oncology floor had no limitation on visiting hours. It meant that you could stay all night. It meant that you had to stay all night.

I walked to the desk. "When do you think my father will wake up?" I asked the nurse, realizing from the look she gave me that it was a loaded question. "I mean from the shot. I thought I'd go get something to eat but if you think he's going to wake up soon I'll wait."

She didn't hesitate, shook her head no. "Go get something to eat," she said. "Take your time. Tenth floor, east. Salad bar's OK but stay away from the soup du jour."

I thanked her. Food was an excuse. I needed to get out of the room for a while and I wanted to call Stan. I headed for the elevator, passing a priest who stood outside room 938B reading from a small black book. People inside the room were crying. The priest looked like an actor backstage waiting for his cue.

I rode the elevator down. Got out on the ground floor where I'd come in only a few hours before. The lobby was expansive and well furnished, comfortingly neutral. Except for the neat rows of wheelchairs, it reminded me of business hotels I'd stayed in, that same shiny anonymity, the big wine-colored couches and framed mirrors, the plate glass windows and blazer-clad receptionists. There was even a gift store selling golf shirts and candy bars. I went in and browsed the magazines and greeting cards. I picked up a spiral notebook and a fingernail file and carried them to the check out counter.

The volunteer at the cash register looked familiar. I probably knew her, I thought. I was in my hometown, three miles from the house I'd grown up in. I'd gone to elementary school and junior high and high school here and she looked like someone who had been in—what? My high school homeroom? Gym class? Maybe senior year. Something about her made me smell chorine, made me think of locker rooms, gym suits and volleyball. Maybe she was one of those student gym leaders who got to blow a shrill referee whistle at slackers like me who couldn't or just wouldn't run fast. She was tall and had the broad shoulders and solid adult physique of someone who as a girl had been athletic. Unlike me. Who had faked menstrual cramps and spent gym class sitting in the bleachers reading paperback novels.

Nancy something. Schroeder, Schneider. Though surely she was married now and had a different last name. She had the plump complacent smoothness of a prosperous housewife with time for virtuous work. She seemed sexless somehow, wholesome, with an efficient short haircut, the opposite of the skanky haggard self I'd seen in the lobby mirrors. She was exactly my age, if this was her, and I supposed that something other than sex grounded her life, children probably. Sex for her had been a means to an end, a stage of life. Married people were like that I thought. They got it over with and moved on. I could see now how that made sense, was efficient. Unlike me, I just kept starting over. I guessed that she had three children, one in high school and two in college by now, as well as a yellow Labrador retriever, an education degree she didn't use, a summerhouse in Leelanau. And a tall perpetually tanned husband, of course, who played golf and was discreet in his infidelities.

I supposed it was an accomplishment, the kind of life I imagined for this woman, an accomplishment I couldn't have appreciated when I was younger. She was the kind of woman my mother would have hated, whose broad backside my father would still make fun of, if he would just wake up. Whatever disappointments and ambivalences she'd suffered were not apparent, were stuffed under all that bustling confident flesh which I suddenly envied. She probably hadn't been up half the night drinking cheap red wine. She rang up my spiral notebook and fingernail file with a kind of good-humored indifference that seemed intended to reform everything around her.

Whoever she was, she hadn't recognized me. No wonder. I glanced again at my reflection in the huge mirror as I left the gift shop. Changed, I thought, imagining myself through Nancy's eyes. I was old or at least I was getting old. My fiftieth birthday had come and gone. My once smooth, high brow was a mess of disorganized wrinkles, gouges ran from the edges of my nose down to my mouth and further, to my jaw, culminating in the beginnings of dewlaps. My neck made me realize why old ladies wore scarves. In ten years if I weren't careful, maybe sooner, I would be a jowly, thick-waisted, coarse-skinned old woman. And that was the least of it; the inner decay was worse. There was this haunted look I was getting, the hooded eyes, the eye bags, the furtive glance, the sunken, set mouth registering decades of disappointment and contrariness.

They should ban reflective surfaces in hospitals I thought. I considered calling Stan but the combined impact of seeing Nancy the rosy-complected gym leader and then my own reflection had unsettled me. Instead I walked back to the east elevator bank and rode up to the tenth floor. The elevator emptied out into a vast stainless steel cafeteria, almost deserted at this time of night except for the night shift staff. It smelled of pizza and sterno gas.

I walked straight past the salad bar and ordered the broccoli soup. The night nurse was right. It was terrible.

CHAPTER 51

Chên / The Arousing (Shock)

The shock of unsettling events brings fear and trembling.
Move toward a higher truth and all will be well.

Eating made me feel more balanced. I decided to call Stan.

"Hey," he said. "How is he?"

"Mad at first, now he's asleep."

"How are you?"

Good question I thought. I didn't know. Numb, for starters, tired, waiting for something to happen, relieved that it felt like something would happen, guilty to feel relieved because the only thing that could happen was not something good yet something I welcomed just for the relief from uneventfulness that the inevitable would offer.

"Okay," I said. "Tired."

"Yeah, it is tiring. I know. I'm sorry."

"How are the dogs?"

"Great. Bob ate two hot dogs and fell right to sleep."

"That's nice. Listen can he stay there a while? I don't know what's going to happen here but it looks like I need to stay."

"Yeah, of course. I already talked to Donna. Clement's OK and she'll keep watching him."

"What are you going to do with the rest of your vacation? Maybe you could do something last-minute with Julie. As far as the clinic knows, you're gone for another five days."

"Not anymore. I'm already back."

"I'm sorry."

"Don't be. I don't mind."

"That's nice."

"Whatever. It's home."

"That's what I mean. You're lucky."

"Come back anytime, Maryanne. The dogs miss you. Do what you need to do and then come back."

CHAPTER 52

Kên / Keeping Still, Mountain

Still your emotions through meditation.

My plan was to move into the hospital. The next morning I took a cab to the house to pick up clothes and to pet Clement, who was glad to see me, rubbing back and forth against my ankles, purring loudly while depositing a thick layer of orange fur on my socks. "Corned beef hash" I could hear him think so I opened a can and gave him a big scoop. I threw my clothes into the washing machine on the short cycle. Took a bath. Threw the clothes in the dryer. Answered some email. Picked up phone messages. Explained in an email to my old boss why I couldn't rewrite a batch of children's hymns by the end of the week to help them get around copyright restrictions. I needed the money but it felt good to say no. Postponed a request for a memorial service from Phillip on behalf of a colleague with an accompanying message from him that said, "I'm telling all my friends you're the go-to gal for this kind of thing."

This kind of thing: Death.

All I'll miss is the animals I thought as I shut down my computer.

Then I remembered Donna had left a phone message saying she would check up on Clement indefinitely and bring in the mail and that I shouldn't worry about stuff. I needed to acknowledge it. Thank her. The thought of her ongoing kindness made my chest ache. I thought of Stan and how he'd been insulted by my gratitude. Why couldn't I just accept kindness, not make a big deal of it? Donna would say gratitude was a distancing technique. That's what he'd meant, it occurred to me now. He'd meant I shouldn't have acted so surprised.

I sat down at my desk, turned my computer back on and typed an email to Donna: "You're the best. Someday I'll try to make it up to you." I deleted it. "Nine bows to you from Zen master Clement. Love, Maryanne ps—C is into corned beef hash these days. I left three cans on the counter."

I couldn't get the tone right, on this or anything else these days. I felt like a fading actor playing a part that used to come naturally. It wasn't that I wasn't sincerely grateful. It's just that I didn't know how to say that without sounding pathetic. Or manipulative. Or flip. Or remote. Maybe I was too sincere. Or just pretending to be sincere. Or maybe I was uncomfortable accepting all this kindness because I was afraid that when the time came to return it I wouldn't be able to. There was a depressing thought. Maybe my problem was that I felt I had to be clever. Cleverly comfortably sincerely grateful. I stared at the message, trying to think of how to rewrite it. The Zen thing was a bit much. I erased the nine bows and then erased the whole thing and wrote, "Thank you from the bottom of my heart, Love, Maryanne." It sounded like a Keepsake Cottage sentiment. I clicked on undo typing and the previous message came up. Weird, yes, but it would have to stand. I pressed send. Donna would forgive it, yet something else I had to be grateful for.

I shut the computer off again, picked up Clement who was sprawled across a pile of unopened mail and gave him one last squeeze. I held him up to my face until I heard him purr, his little motor thrumming through his thick soft coat, which was the color of a Dreamsicle. He placed one paw softly on my cheek and looked into my eyes.

"How's Frank?" he said. Frank was my father.

"Not so good," I said. "I think he's dying."

Clement continued to stare at me, his big yellow eyes knowing death well. "I liked him," he said.

He blinked slowly, his yellow eyes squeezing shut then open again. "He was generous to me." Then he pressed his paws gently against my chest, floated up out of my arms, hopped to the floor and slipped past me down the basement stairs to look for spiders. I dragged my duffle bag out the door.

I was still packed for camping and anything that wasn't in the bag I could buy at the gift shop. Somewhere in there would be a clean pair of jeans and about a week's worth of underwear. My fleece jacket still smelled like smoke but who cared. All the camping food was still in Stan's car but I'd ransacked the kitchen and took what I had, a bag of unsalted almonds and a Milky Way. To these I'd added a yellow legal pad and the *I Ching*. I tossed the bag in my trunk and headed back to the hospital.

Chapter 53

Chien / Development
(Gradual Progress)

Those who persevere make continuous progress

I'd been camped in my father's hospital room for four days and they still hadn't been able to wake him up from what they were initially calling an induced coma. Now it was just a coma. On the fifth morning his doctor stopped by to tell me that my father was in stage four metastasized cancer and that he recommended palliative care.

"Do you have a DNR order," he asked, not looking at me.

Do not resuscitate. Yes, I said. My father had handled this all three years ago during a spasm of efficiency in a rare moment of acknowledgement of the possibility of his own passing. DNR, will, power of attorney. His legal and financial life was in surprisingly good shape for a man who refused to believe he would ever die. He'd paid off the house decades earlier, he had long-term care insurance, there was a cemetery plot all ready for him next to my mother with his name on the tombstone waiting for the second date to be carved in after the hyphen. It was only his body that was in chaos. Shutting down is what the doctor called it.

"I'm recommending that we move him. Upstairs," he said, lending special weight to the word.

I must have registered incomprehension because then he added, "To the hospice floor."

"Ah," I said, "You mean you don't expect him to recover."

"Yes and no," the doctor said, brightening at the opportunity to explain. "He may regain consciousness but he's not going to improve significantly. We could pump him full of drugs, maybe prolong his death. But we're not going to prolong his life." He smiled at me, reasonably. "If you know what I mean. This way we'll just give him what he needs to be comfortable and if he wakes up he won't be in pain. He might even be able to talk."

"You're telling me he's dying."

"Well, yes. But he'll continue to have some quality of life up until his death."

This was the first time anyone had used the word death in my father's presence and now the doctor had used it twice. I didn't speak of it around my father. The word offended him and I understood. I glanced over at him, afraid he'd heard and would rise up in bed to protest. Instead he just lay there, uncharacteristically silent.

"I don't want to stop treatment unless, you know, there really isn't anything else to do." I waited for the doctor to say something. He didn't. "I mean, a week ago he was OK. A month ago he was cooking corned beef hash. Out of a can, but still, with scrambled eggs." The doctor raised an eyebrow. Moving him upstairs seemed like a personal defeat for both of us, like giving up.

"I understand," the doctor said. "I'm just telling you the options. We'll continue watching him but I recommend that you consider hospice care. Some people find it a wonderful way to say goodbye. Take your time and think it over. We'd remove all the IVs, and just use minimal means to keep him comfortable. Morphine is a blessing in these cases."

These cases. He smiled again and squeezed my shoulder. Speaking this language about these matters must make it all much easier I thought. Blessing, say goodbye, palliative care, quality of life, options, comfortable. What vague, consoling words. Morphine at least packed some punch. The doctor was young and ruddy-faced, blithely confident, with a full head of coarse blond hair and blindingly white teeth. Just looking at him made me feel tired. Together, I thought, the doctor, my father and I represented three of the seven ages of man in this room alone. The trappings had changed since Shakespeare but the last act remained the same. Sans everything.

The doctor's rubber-soled shoes squeaked as he strode energetically out of the room, a moistly fragrant whiff of antiseptic soap rising from his flapping scrubs. I supposed if you were doing your best to help you could move like that, guiltlessly, decisively. It must be nice I thought. It was the opposite for me. I shuffled, guilty and indecisive and stiff from sleeping in chairs. I had nothing to do. Or nothing I could do that was of any help. All I did was sit there. And for what? To be there if he woke up I told myself. Or to make a decision if something happened and I was expected to decide. Decide what, though? The papers were signed, the game was over. It didn't seem fair; he would want another at-bat.

So there I sat, keeping him company, in case he noticed. A person wouldn't want to be alone at a time like this. I wondered, if he did wake up, if he'd be happy to see me or if he'd be disappointed it wasn't Susan, if he hoped to be reunited with someone else, here or in the beyond. My mother? His mother? His grandparents? Some old girlfriend? His childhood chums? Dead pets? There had to be someone he'd rather see than me but, as I sat there watching him breathe, the blue veins under the paper-thin skin on his eyes pulsing faintly, I couldn't think of who it was, and it seemed like yet another failure of mine that I didn't know.

Of course I'd called Susan in Minneapolis. She'd sounded annoyed. It was inconvenient, I acknowledged. She was planning to come she said but doubted it was as serious as I claimed. I was a drama queen she reminded me and he was a tough old bird. She chuckled affectionately at the lovable sitcom family she'd invented for herself. Then she stopped chuckling and said she'd look at the airfares though her column was due tomorrow and it didn't give her much slack for travel. She'd phased out of daily reporting and now wrote a twice-weekly slice of life column for *The Minneapolis Star Tribune* which had won awards for its humorous yet warmly philosophical take on relationships and daily life. Plus, she said, her in-laws were there and she felt she needed to lend moral support to her husband. It upset him when they visited.

"He's dying," I said. I felt sorry for myself, for him, even for her. "If you want to see him before he goes I think this is it." Silence. "And I don't think he should be alone." I added that last part because I didn't have the nerve to say what I meant, that I didn't want to be alone.

"He's not alone," she said. "He's got you."

"Right. I've got to go," I said and hung up.

She was right, it turned out, though without knowing how right. He wasn't alone. After a couple of days of pounding on the door and not getting an answer, the neighbors figured out what was going on, made some calls to the local hospitals and to each other and began showing up.

All the names I'd heard in stories, the names attached to notes in disposable plastic food containers, suddenly became attached to women and a few men who arrived with flowers, candy, homemade cards from their children, teddy bears, Tupperware dishes full of cookies, brownies, toffee and prune kollachkes.

When I got back from talking with Susan, I found a sallow broad-faced blond woman in a rhinestone-studded denim jacket, tight jeans and high heels sitting in the orange chair next to his bed. "He loves these," she confided in me over the kollachkes, an intimate glint shining in her welling eyes. "They make him go. He wrote a poem about it."

Then: "You must be the daughter?" She looked me up and down appraisingly, lingering on my grimy hiking boots.

"Ah," she said in her Baltic accent, as a tight, knowing movement that might have been the afterbirth of an aborted smile animated the corners of her mouth. The dirty boots had triggered a memory. "He mentioned your dog to me."

The kollachke lady—her name was Martina—came every day after that, always with food, and sat silently sometimes; other times she read to him from the newspaper. There was an old guy in a dirty sweat suit from the YMCA pool who brought a tin pie pan full of homemade venison jerky and the neighbors from across the alley who brought pictures of their grandchildren. Here was my father's real life, laid bare, worlds away from our stilted visits. These, his neighbors, expected nothing in particular from him but simply loved him for the occasional joke or story over a returned piece of mis-delivered mail and a shared plate of sugar cookies. That was our problem, I thought. We expected too much from one another, we had disappointed each other too often and too deeply. We had worn each other out with our expectations and had nothing more to say. These easy well-defined relationships were the late fulfillment of his life, the improvement on his earlier frustrated efforts to connect with us, his family. My mother, my sister, me—we never quite fit him. None of us had satisfied his raging need for an appreciative audience. But as soon as he gave up on us these kind people arrived with food and flirtation, and no agenda. They were his living circle, his real family, now.

"Do you want to be alone with him for a minute?" I asked the woman sitting in a cloud of perfume and hairspray with tears in her eyes and the plate of kollachkes on her lap.

She softened, blushed. "Would you mind?' she said.

I took a walk.

CHAPTER 54

Kuei Mei / The Marrying Maiden

In relationships, desires lead to misfortune.
Behave with discipline and balance.

William Faulkner said somewhere that the past isn't dead, it isn't even past. I'm afraid he's right though I try to believe otherwise. It doesn't match up with my Zen aspirations, my effort to live in the present.

I'd spent my whole life reliving and revising my past, stirring it into the present, never setting it down and walking away. Being in the hospital day after day made it even worse. Being there was like being launched into orbit around my own life, which I recircled endlessly, like it was a nearby planet, visible yet unreachable and happening all at once. I looked down on my house, my animals, my father, my family, a sequence of boyfriends, teachers, cars, apartments, jobs, all the clothes I'd ever worn. A yellow blouse I'd loved in high school sailed by along with a half-sized rented violin I never learned to play and the skinny polka dot belt I'd left in a hotel room once by mistake in the heat of a love affair lunch date. Here they lived on in an eternal present. A plum colored jumper from seventh grade flapped by like an elegant bird, the memory of its color and smooth knit fabric as sharp as a taste, and thinking of its perfect A-line skirt and the periwinkle blue blouse I'd wore under it gave me a sensation in my throat somewhere between vomit and orgasm. From up here in outer space my relationships with Stan and Phillip and Mr. Payne and the Sunday school teacher who'd reached under my skirt and kissed me behind the baptismal were equidistant, all equally remote, all equally important and all equally bungled by me. And I didn't just repeat the memories. I tinkered with them, I relived them differently, re-imagining conversations, re-explaining myself so that these phantoms would finally be convinced of my point of view and settle back into their place in line. They say that when you die your life passes in front of your eyes but what they don't tell you is that the same thing happens when your father dies.

CHAPTER 55

Fêng / Abundance (Fullness)

A moment of great influence is at hand.
Prepare wisely and act accordingly.

After seven days, with my assent, they moved my father upstairs. I insisted on an IV for morphine and the availability of oxygen. Choking, I'd heard, was terrifying and miserable enough to wake you up just long enough to experience your own horrible death. All other support was removed.

It was a different world up here, easier, quieter. It was like a rehearsal for heaven. The walls were painted yellow. The lights were blessedly dim, the nurses eerily good-natured. No one ran. No one moaned. Unlike the overworked rushed brusque agitated and over-caffeinated crew downstairs, poking and prodding and avoiding eye contact as they inflicted pain, these nurses, mostly women, seemed almost euphorically content. They smiled at me and at my father, brought me tea and blankets, rubbed his back and washed him head to foot as soon as we moved in, after firmly directing me out of the room and into the lounge where I was assigned a plate of ginger cookies to eat.

The effort going on downstairs to shore up the breached banks of old sick bodies, to fix, cure, change, heal against all odds, the sickening tension, that mandate to do something dramatic, desperate: all that was absent here. The doctors rarely visited; we lost causes were happily safe from their heroics. The nurses handled everything that mattered. Here it was all gentle pats and smiling acceptance. I wanted to move in and never leave.

My father's room was equipped with a small dresser and a bathroom with a shower. Not all hospice patients were unconscious or immobile and they could enjoy these niceties but since my father couldn't, I had dibs. The bathroom was cleaner than mine at home with no dogs or cats lining up to drink out of the tub and it had better water pressure. We moved in as if into a hotel room, my comatose roommate and me.

I began to think of us as roommates. It was our room, we enjoyed daily newspaper deliveries, we were ready for dinner. They brought us my father's portions of hospital food on trays and it seemed so unnatural for him not to eat, even now, that I asked them to continue. What if he woke up and found out I'd cancelled his food while buying my own upstairs? I couldn't do it so I ate his on a tray beside his bed. I ate it all including bland watery soup and packaged pudding. The terrible food didn't matter. Now that my father was no longer arguing with me and now that the violent ministrations to his body had stopped I found it peaceful to sit here with him, reading, napping, sipping tasteless food from plastic bowls. Sometimes Martina, the kollachke lady, joined us. We took turns reading out loud to him. When he and I were alone I talked to him about the food.

"You'd like this corn chowder, Dad," I heard myself say one afternoon. "It's like the kind you make but it isn't as good. I don't think they use real bacon. Or cream. Actually you might not like it." Why couldn't I have been such a good friend to him when he was conscious, I wondered. It was true that he made excellent corn chowder and I wondered exactly how he did it and if I'd ever mentioned it to him.

When we first moved in, Tony, the one male nurse, had wheeled in an over-upholstered recliner for me to sleep in, anticipating I'd be there awhile. The veins that popped up on his scrawny pale arms matched his lavender scrubs as he pushed the huge chair into position, and the bumpy scars that stood up along the purple veins suggested either regular meds or a bad habit. I wondered if his shaved head was a condition or a fashion statement. Or maybe it was an expression of solidarity with his bald cancer patients. Not that my father had lost any hair. It had been too late for chemo and he didn't want it anyway. His full head of white hair had been his sustaining vanity in old age and now it fanned out on the pillow behind him like a slightly yellowed aura against the bleached hospital linens, the last physical part of him to remain vital.

"Anyone else coming?" Tony had asked. I felt embarrassed to say no and reflexively checked his gaunt face for irony but we were in heaven now and I saw only helpfulness. "I could put another chair right here," he offered, indicating the empty space by the window. I had a momentary vision of Stan and me sleeping side by side on plaid recliners, dozing as my father passed peacefully into the next world, and then closing the door and climbing into one together to respond to death in the only way that made sense. I put the thought out of my mind.

"Maybe my sister will come," I said. Last time I'd spoken to Susan she was still checking fares. I sounded pathetic.

"Relax, dear, it's going to be OK," he said, positioning himself behind me and kneading my shoulders with his surprisingly strong hands. "I'll bring the other one over later, just in case." Did he wink? Had he read my mind?

As it turned out, Donna showed up that afternoon just as Tony was settling the second recliner into place, patting the extra blankets he'd brought with it.

"Sistuh!" he greeted her, pursing his lips and striking a pose as he noted her overalls, combat boots and gray crew cut.

"Sistuh but not sister," I said. "Dear friend." I hugged her. I'd been hugging all kinds of people lately. I'd hugged Tony earlier in the day. Ordinarily I was not a hugger or even a toucher but my defenses were down. Normal physical boundaries didn't seem to exist here. Hugging was the least of it. People were handling my father's body as if he were a cherished infant. I seldom hugged Donna and it was like hugging a man, somebody's retired policeman uncle. She was huge and covered with a soft layer of fat but underneath there was solid muscle. The buckles of her overalls smashed cold against my cheek.

"Thanks for coming" I said. "How did you find us?"

"I figured," she said, hauling an old green backpack off her shoulder. "Look. I brought stuff."

She had brought a feast.

She unloaded cloth napkins, brownies, a block of cheddar, crackers, a still-warm baguette, grapes, M&Ms, little bottles of fruit juice and a plastic container full of macaroni and cheese.

"For him," she said, patting the container and nodding towards my father. "You know, something soft, just in case."

"In case of what?"

We stared at each over the macaroni. "You know. In case he improves."

We let that thought hang in the air as we looked at him. He didn't look like someone who would ever again want to eat macaroni and cheese, but there were no limits to Donna's belief that she could fix the world.

"Stan says hi," she said. "He's worried about you but he doesn't want to bother you."

"I miss the animals," I said.

"He misses you."

"Ladies?" Tony had left and returned with a tray table, which he set between the recliners.

"Join us, Tony?"

"Don't mind if I do," he said.

My Father's Corn Chowder

Boil 4 large cut-up potatoes in real chicken stock if you have it. Otherwise use bouillon.

When potatoes are soft mash them coarsely. Turn down heat to simmer.

Add a quart of half and half. (That's my father talking. I use whole milk.)

Add a large can of corn, regular or creamed, depending.

Cook ½ pound bacon separately until crisp. Crumble it up and add to soup.

Cook some chopped green onions in the bacon fat and add to soup.

Add some cut-up celery.

Add some flour to thicken.

Add lots of black pepper. Garnish with parsley.

Serve with a double martini.

CHAPTER 56

Lü / The Wanderer

We are all wanderers in the Unknown.
Those who travel beside the Sage
are protected from harm.

The next afternoon I was napping in one of the big chairs when I was awakened by voices and the smell of oregano outside the door. It opened a crack and I saw Tony poking his head in to scan the room. Looming behind him, wider and taller, was Donna holding a pizza box. She was wearing a fresh pair of overalls, this one with yellow paw prints embroidered across the bib.

Then the door opened wider and there stood Stan holding Bob on a leash. Bob was wearing a harness and a red nylon vest and was straining against the leash to get into the room.

Stan let go and Bob galloped over to me, in full body wag, then rushed to the bed to sniff my father. I grabbed him by the hindquarters and buried my head in his exhilaratingly shampoo-scented fur. Stan had given him a bath.

"Excuse me, ma'am," Stan said. "Please don't touch the service dog."

"Where did you get the outfit? It looks real."

"Close enough," he said looking as smug as I'd ever seen him. "It's a canine life jacket. Got it at the boat supply store—so your dog doesn't sink. He likes wearing it."

I unsnapped the leash and Bob raced around the room, inspecting every surface for scents, and then, as if on cue and without prompting, hauled himself up on the high hospital bed and settled himself carefully alongside my father so that his back touched the length of his body but didn't press down on him. Bob outweighed him now and he seemed to understand he needed to be careful. I glanced at Tony and he shrugged, rolling his eyes to the ceiling as he unloaded the twenty-pound bag of large-breed anti-itch formula dog food from the seat of the wheelchair they'd brought it up in.

"I have no idea how all that black hair got into this bed," he said.

"Time to eat," Stan said, unzipping a cooler. "Wine, beer anyone? Orange Crush?"

"You guys think of everything."

Tony and Donna agreed they both needed to leave after the first bottle of wine, Donna to get home to her own dog and Tony to get back to work. Stan, who had been standing next to the bed feeding pizza crust to Bob, followed them to the door, host-like.

Tony said not to worry about Bob being there and that he'd tell the other on-duty nurse and didn't think she'd mind. "It won't be an issue unless one of the doctors comes in and then Stan just has to pretend he's blind."

"Epileptic," Stan said. "Bob is playing the part of a seizure-sensing dog."

"Works for me. All that thrashing, so manly."

Stan gave a little wave and Tony and Donna headed out.

"He has a crush on you," I said when we were alone.

"He just likes my shoes."

"They are very nice shoes," I said. Then, "Thanks for doing this."

"Don't mention it. Although these pizzas did cost me thirty-eight dollars. Donna insisted on the works. Actually Donna set it up. We'll have to get him out of here at some point, though, to pee. And then back in again."

"You mean if he stays the night."

"That's what I mean."

CHAPTER 57

Sun / The Gentle
(The Penetrating, Wind)

*Consistent correctness turns every situation
to your advantage.*

As it turned out the nurses liked having Bob there. They brought him treats from uneaten patient meals and filled his bowl with fresh water whenever they stopped in, showering him with the same beneficent attention they paid to the rest of us. They showed Stan how to get him in and out of the hospital on the same schedule as the pediatric therapy dogs and for the next few days he spent most of his time lying calmly in bed next to my father or being walked by one of the nurses. He lengthened himself along-side my father's shrunken body, making as much surface contact as he could. He seemed to know exactly what he was there to do and when he needed to stretch or scratch—an energetic leg thumping procedure that involved vigorous bouts of rocking and vibrating as well as some growly ass-gnawing—he removed himself to the pile of purple blankets Tony had left for him on the floor.

Stan came and went, commuting between the clinic, his house and my father's hospital room. Sometimes he spent the night there in the second recliner, which he swore was more comfortable than his own bed, or brought paperwork and carryout food in the evening after the clinic closed and then went home to his own dogs.

We settled into a companionable routine, dozing side by side on the brown plaid recliners just as I'd imagined, not talking much. It was Stan's ability to not talk but simply radiate a reassuring silence that I found most comforting. His response to emergency was calm and efficient, perhaps a natural gift or maybe just a result of years of working with stressed, miserable dogs and cats who needed a soothing hand.

Once my father opened his eyes and announced in a raspy annoyed-sounding voice to no one I could see, "I will join you shortly," and then shut his eyes and sighed as if he'd been interrupted at something taxing. Another time he opened his eyes, blew a kiss toward the ceiling and began to choke. He looked afraid. Bob sat up, ears erect, chest out, and placed a paw on his chest, staring first into my father's unfocused eyes and then up at the ceiling in the direction of the blown kiss. Stan vaulted out of his chair and stood on the other side of the bed gripping my father's hand in his. I stood at the foot of the bed and watched. Neither of us mentioned calling the nurse or spoke at all. Pretty soon the choking stopped and my father relaxed and seemed to go back to sleep. Bob relaxed too, setting his head back down on the covers between his paws, while Stan returned to his recliner and resumed reading the latest issue of *Veterinary Practice*.

"Can't Stan help him get this over with?" It was Bob.

"What?" I telegraphed back, shocked, but not wanting to speak out loud.

"He does it to dogs and cats all the time. I hate to see him suffer like this."

"We don't do it to people."

"Poor people," he said, settling his big head gloomily down on his paws.

CHAPTER 58

Tui / The Joyous, Lake

True joy is experienced by those who are
strong within and gentle without.

Susan arrived nine days after I called, managing to look glamorous, tragic, guilty and put out all at once. She came directly from the airport, her wiry little body draped with soft luggage and dragging a suitcase on wheels. She was wearing a short jacketed olive green cashmere pantsuit cut to look like pajamas, square toed boots and a green and pumpkin colored striped scarf wrapped several times around her ropy throat. Her curly dark blond hair was pinned up and springing out into coils around her flushed bony face, her thickly framed turquoise blue reading glasses slipped attractively down her nose. She was adorable in disarray. She announced her arrival by dropping all her luggage on the floor at once with a thump that made Bob start.

After an emotional outburst at the sight of the patient—"dear God, so frail!"—and a sniffing dismissal of Bob—"yours I suppose?"—she took a cab to our father's house and moved in, immediately setting up her laptop at the Formica kitchen table after she stripped it of its plastic tablecloth. Here she planned to continue work on her newspaper column while mounting a cleaning, purging and reassigning of assets campaign punctuated with daily visits to sit at my father's bedside to cry and make to-do lists.

"I can't believe the things I'm finding," she said in a breathy, ominous whisper one afternoon. I just raised my eyebrows. These bedside chats made me nervous.

"I pitched the porn. Though it's ancient." She said this matter-of-factly, as if its antiquity somehow defused it. We'd just had lunch and she was reapplying orange lipstick while staring at her reflection in the convex surface of a hospital spoon she'd polished with the corner of a sheet from my father's bed. "Oh don't look so shocked. That's nothing. But there are all of these letters. From women. Lots of them. They all appear to be in love with him."

"You mean the food ladies?"

"Food schmood. Who's Martina?"

"She's the kollachke lady," I said. "She was his cleaning lady for a while I think. She comes here every day to see him." She and I had become friendly, though we didn't talk much, and she seemed to have forgiven me my shoes. I always left her alone with him, with her holding his hand, after accepting one of the pastries she brought me daily. "You'll meet her if you stay."

"I don't want to meet her," Susan said. "She wrote him a love poem."

"Really. Really?"

I had intended to stay out of this but I couldn't help but be intrigued. I knew about the food for haiku exchange but this sounded like something of a different order. Maybe Susan was exaggerating. But maybe not. How did the old man do it? How did he stay in the game, that mean old man, and still manage to inspire so much love? I led her into the hall.

"Is there one special one? Or just a fan club?"

"Maybe both. But I'm working on finding that out."

"You mean you're going through his stuff?"

"Of course. Listen, there are these weird writings of his. And money everywhere in envelopes, tucked into books. Not a lot, usually. Fifteen dollars here, twelve dollars there, but listen. Some of it's in dictionaries or in the encyclopedia, tucked into the page where the word money appears or currency or cash or, in the dictionary of slang?, under jack. Can you believe it? And under windfall? There was a wad of hundreds. And a lotto ticket."

"How many hundreds?"

"Twelve. Twelve one hundred dollar bills."

I laughed.

"You laugh but these are things we have to deal with. We have to check every page of every book. Here," she said. She dug into her purse and handed me a wad of bills held together by a rubber band. "Here's half of what I've found so far." I counted it. Finally, new tires, I thought.

"And these weird writings of his, it seems like some romance novel slash cookbook, with drawings. I'm reading everything. Apparently he was trying to get it published. There's a whole correspondence about some automatic vibrating potato peeler thing he invented that he was trying to get a patent for. And some vegetable-based skin cream for breast enlargement he was cooking up in the kitchen for God's sake out of rutabagas and molasses or something. Apparently he was having the neighbors test it and was keeping notes on their success. There's a chart, for Christ's sake."

"Oh that," I said.

"You knew about that?"

"Well sort of." I was embarrassed to remember it. "Susan, he's not dead yet. You know him. He could sit up and walk out of here tomorrow. He'll be furious."

"Oh don't be such a fucking scaredy cat goody goody. Such a self-sacrificing sad sack, so shocked. You go over there every other day for years with your little casseroles and you don't notice this shit? Even if he does wake up, which he won't, he's not going back to that house. There are fourteen stairs down to the basement—I counted—down to his mushroom farm, did you know about that? Six stairs just to get from the back door down to the sidewalk. We have to figure out what to do."

I didn't say anything but I knew she was right.

"You know as well as I do he's not going home," she continued. "I hired cleaners but the house is still a mess. And I'm trying to work. I'm throwing everything out I can and there's a huge pile of stuff for you to look over. Anything you don't want I'll pitch. I took a few little things. I didn't think you'd mind. I thought I'd take Grammy's rocker. Unless you want it.

Actually I already shipped it home. But the paper. God, we have to go through it at least enough to know what we're throwing out."

The thought of going through everything was sickening. Apparently he had saved every letter ever sent him, recorded every penny he had ever spent. He believed in keeping track of things, thought us slovenly for not doing so. I thought of throwing away all the effort in those decades of careful accounting at his old desk with the little cubbyholes and tiny drawers good for nothing but stamps. I thought of the basement full of shoeboxes crammed with letters tied with string. I thought of the closet full of old clothes, carefully mended, by him, and washed a thousand times in an age when it was cheaper and faster just to throw them out and buy new. I thought of the vases full of years-old dried up bouquets he wouldn't throw out, the empty cookie tins and recycled wrapping paper. I thought of his tidbit projects, as he called them, his inventions, lined up on cookie sheets and pie pans in the pantry, all labeled with cryptic notes written on the backs of envelopes and the piles of yellow legal pads full of cramped writing I'd averted my eyes from all these years. Why hadn't he told me about his projects? Why hadn't I asked?

Of course she was right. Saving it wouldn't matter to him once he was dead. It would be no monument to him, just a pile of worn-out stuff. Sooner or later we had to do something about it. It made me think of my own house, ten years' worth of stuff that Phillip had just walked away from. I should be grateful to Susan. At least she was dealing with that.

CHAPTER 59

Huan / Dispersion (Dissolution)

Disperse hard attitudes with gentleness.

My father died a week later, on a Thursday morning, around ten o'clock. Susan was at the house, meeting with realtors. Stan was at the clinic. Tony had the day off. Donna was in the gift shop visiting Nancy. Bob and I were alone with him, me in the plaid recliner and Bob stretched out as usual in the bed with his long back flat against my father's small body, his black fur against the white sheets looking like an oil spill in the snow. We had dispensed with the red service vest, Velcroing it back on only when we took him in and out of the hospital room for walks. No one seemed to care that he was here and I thought the body contact was good for them both.

I was in the big chair reading my horoscope in the *Chicago Sun-Times* when I heard a commotion coming from the bed. When I looked up I saw that Bob had scrambled into his alert sphinx position, chest out and ears up, and was making a low growling sound in his throat while staring into my father's face. He threw his head back and switched to a soft howl that sounded like a yodel or an attempt to articulate words. Then he stopped that and just stared, ears raised in hyper listening position. My father's intensely blue eyes were open and staring back at Bob. He was smiling.

I walked to the side of the bed and did what Stan had done. I took his hand and held it. It was cold and I couldn't feel a pulse. At my touch he slowly turned his head away from Bob and looked at me, a kind of sleepy, amused wonder in his eyes, no pain, and then turned back to stare at Bob. He appeared to relax then and grew very still. His hand grew colder. His breathing stilled. We remained like that for some time and then Bob's ears suddenly drooped. He looked at me.

"He's gone," he said.

I looked at my father. His dry lips were white and slightly parted, his jaw stiff. His open-eyed blue gaze was frozen in Bob's direction.

"He says thank you," Bob said, clear as a bell somewhere between my brain and my ears. "And he sends his love to Martina. And to you and Susan and Clement and Gregoire. And Gretchen."

"Who's Gretchen?" I said out loud.

But after silently delivering this astonishing piece of news Bob went back to being just a dog. He lumbered off the high bed, stiffly, ass in the air and one leg at a time, favoring his bad back hip. Then he stretched, lapped up some water, even wagged his tail in rhythm to his gulps, and lay down on his pile of purple blankets and began to scratch. He was not sad; he was finished. He had done his job, had conveyed my father from this life to the next and now both their long hard jobs were done.

I sat with my father, first holding his ice-cold hand and then not, for another hour or so until the nurse came to check on us.

"He's gone," I said, quoting Bob.

She leaned over and looked at him with great tenderness, touching his face as if I'd told her that he was cold. She ran her hand gently over his forehead and took his hand and felt his wrist for a pulse.

"Yes, he is," she said. "He's gone." Then she smiled, at him, and closed his eyes.

CHAPTER 60

Chieh / Limitation

Voluntarily chosen limits empower your growth.

When I called Susan and told her the news she wept loudly. I asked if she wanted to come over and view the body, say goodbye. She sighed loudly and said no, that she wanted to remember him as he was in life and that work would be her tribute. She was writing a series of dispatches for her newspaper called "A Death in the Family" that were featured daily on page two and ran along with a forty-year-old photo of Susan and my father with their arms around each other standing in front of a Christmas tree.

I was both relieved and disappointed she wasn't coming. I sat in my father's room, with his body, until they took him away, and then I stayed on pretending to collect his things, though there weren't many, until the cleaning crew came to strip the bed. The removal of the body had been as uneremonious and efficient as the removal of the bed linens; this room that had been our sanctuary was now being prepared for someone else. It was time for us to leave. I Velcroed Bob back into his red vest, packed up my father's few belongings along with what remained of Bob's food and left, pocketing a jar of hand cream from the bedside table as a souvenir on my way out. I took Bob to the car, which had been sitting in the hospital parking lot all this time, and settled him in the back seat. Then I went back inside, to the gift shop, and bought one last newspaper from Nancy. I rode the elevator upstairs to the cafeteria and bought a cup of tea and some French fries and sat at my favorite window table one last time and ate the French fries and read the newspaper. Then I wrapped up what was left of the fries in a paper napkin for Bob. It was time to leave the hospital but I didn't want to. It had come to feel like home.

When I arrived at my father's house I found Susan sitting at the kitchen table talking with my father's minister on her cell phone. She had definite ideas about the funeral and I was happy to let her take over.

When she got off the phone she told me to sit down. She had something to tell me, she said. She'd found the will.

"We already have the will," I said. "He sent us both a copy three years ago."

"This one is updated," she said. "You might want to take a look."

CHAPTER 61

Chung Fu / Inner Truth

Through openness and gentleness
the correct solution is reached.

Gretchen turned out to be Martina's eight-year-old daughter, a wan gap-toothed child with dishwater blond hair whose photo we found in my father's wallet. She had a talent for drawing horses, many renditions of which were stacked neatly in his bottom desk drawer along with her report card and a Valentine she'd made. She was named in the will along with Martina; each of them was to receive a quarter of my father's estate. Gretchen's share was to be placed in a trust to be made available at age eighteen and applied to her college education or held until she was twenty-five if she did not choose to attend college. Susan and I were to split the other half. We were, however, the sole heirs to all royalties from his inventions and his literary estate.

"So is this darling Gretchen person our half sister?" Susan demanded, holding the corner of the little school picture with the very tips of her perfectly French-manicured fingers as if she meant to touch it with as little of her flesh as possible. I was sitting at the kitchen table while Susan paced up and down the narrow space between the counter and the stove. "Is that what we are to understand? That we are related to this little nebbish? This troll? Are we in fact one big happy family?"

Susan was very upset. The will was spread out across the bare table; gone was the plastic tablecloth with the pictures of sunflowers on it. Gone also were the grocery store coupons and little notes my father had written to himself and kept tucked between the sugar bowl and the saltshaker. Gone likewise were the pictures of the neighbors' grandchildren and the promotional magnets in the shape of houses and pizzas that had held them on the refrigerator door. Susan had gone on a cleaning rampage, clearing out as much of him as she could.

"Is that what we are to understand?" she repeated, louder, waving the little picture in my face.

"No. I don't think so. I don't know. Maybe. Actually I have no idea. But I don't think so. Maybe she's a surrogate grandchild. He was pretty pissed off we didn't come up with any."

"What do you mean? He was perfectly happy not having them."

"Are you kidding? He was furious." I thought of the not-so-subtle insinuations he'd made about Susan and me, implying what slackers he thought we were for failing to reproduce. "You weren't here. I took the brunt of it."

She ignored this. "We'll have it overturned. I'm sure it's easily done."

I didn't say anything. It seemed wrong somehow to overrule someone's last wishes, though whether it was any worse than stiffing your children in the will in favor of people unknown to them I wasn't sure. Unless Gretchen was his child. Either way it was his money, or had been. And, to be fair, he hadn't stiffed us, just halved our inheritance, made it less decisive. I didn't dare to express any of these vacillations to Susan, who was shaking by now.

"How dare he let us sit there caring for him, weeping for him, tending him devotedly in his old age and his time of weakness and then turn around and pull this crap from the grave!"

"Susan, you didn't do any of those things."

"Well technically no but you did. How do you feel?"

Numb as usual would have been the truthful answer but I tried to rouse myself to Susan's level of angst. "I feel kind of, well, pretty bad. But that's not the point. Or not the only point. And we don't need the money, really. Especially you. We'll live."

Susan launched the little picture like a Frisbee. It landed in Bob's water dish where it made a small inconsequential splash. "When if ever will you stop being so goddamned wishy-washy mealy-mouthed blah blah blah-ish? You are feckless! When will you stop all this on the one hand this and on the other hand that crappy bullshit! It's bullshit! Don't you dare tell me you're not as mad as I am. You just won't admit it because it makes you feel morally superior you're so fucking goody goody, such a goddamned goody fucking goody two shoes. And it's all bullshit anyway, you who just dumped her cold-blooded mannequin of a boyfriend and quit her job to create some whimsical bullshit of a fake business while fucking the cute horse doctor with those hairy handsome hands of his knowing very well you only had to wait and the money would be yours. Well ha ha it's not!"

She was sincerely weeping now, differently than she had at my father's bedside, weeping with genuine, wild grief as she stamped her feet and paced aerobically up and down the length of the cramped kitchen, the ropes on her neck throbbing as she bumped into furniture and boxes she'd already packed and labeled. She paused occasionally to pound on the old table at the exact place where my father used to pound it during his dinnertime diatribes.

"That's not what I did," I said. "That's not at all what happened. And don't call me feckless."

"He was withholding and stingy my whole life," she sobbed. "He withheld money and praise and love and everything that mattered and now he pulls this crap."

"But you were his favorite," I said.

She stopped crying and looked at me, pleased. "You think so?" Then she looked away. "We were planning to retire on that money."

"It's OK, Susan," I said, thinking of the definitive way Bob had communicated the names to me, in order. I couldn't go against that, as much out of respect for Bob as for my father. "Things will work out."

"You are such a wimp," she said, blowing her nose as she fished the little picture of Gretchen out of the water bowl and fed it into the garbage disposal she'd had installed.

CHAPTER 62

Hsiao Kuo / Preponderance of the Small

*In a great storm the wise bird returns to her nest
and waits patiently.*

Two weeks after my father died, immediately after the funeral and the buffet lunch at the house, we held a memorial fundraiser in the back yard for Angels, to benefit the feral cat stay-and-spay project they were launching and to beef up their foster dog program for hard-to-place-pups. It was Donna's idea. It could be an annual event in my father's honor, she said. It turned out he'd been sending her donations for her various fundraisers for years.

The idea was to auction off what was left of the contents of the house plus anything else anyone wanted to donate. Tony agreed to be the auctioneer and we invited everybody at the funeral plus everyone on Bonnie's Friends and Angels mailing list. At first Susan was against it but since Donna, Stan and I said we'd do all the work she gave in, especially when we explained we'd have it catered and planned to hire Nancy, the gift shop volunteer Donna had fallen for, to be the bartender. I think Susan realized she could work it into *Daily Dispatches from the Edge of Beyond*, her working title for the book she planned to get out of her "A Death in the Family" columns.

The auction was a success. Susan burst into tears whenever an especially high bid was made and everyone agreed Nancy looked great in a tuxedo. We raised over two thousand dollars for the shelter and split it right down the middle—half for the feral cats and half for the hard-to-place-pups.

CHAPTER 63

Chi Chi / After Completion

Good fortune unfolds for those who remain on guard
against inferior influences.

Seven months later, after we'd settled the will, found an agent willing to take on my father's cookbook and sold his house, I sold mine, picket fence and all. When I put it on the market Stan suggested I move in with him. I said I didn't think I wanted to live in the same house where he'd lived with his wife. He said he'd been meaning to sell it and we could buy something together. I said I'd think about it.

I put the house on the market the day after Bob died. Bob's decline happened suddenly, inevitably. One day I'd bent down to take off his leash and felt a hard lump on his chest. I squeezed it and he looked me in the eye and said, "This is it. Tell Stan." I called Stan and he checked it out. Bob was right. Cancer. Three weeks after that he stopped eating. He lost fourteen pounds. His ribs stuck out the way they had when he was a scrawny puppy, fresh from the shelter. It became harder and harder for him to get up, go out to pee, sleep though the night. Our walks stopped. He smelled bad. He couldn't get in and out of the bed without Stan lifting him and even then he cried out. I couldn't lift him myself. On nights Stan didn't sleep over I pulled his bed next to mine and he slept there, or tried to, with my hand dangling over the edge grazing his fur until my arm went numb. Clement sat by his side at night. Stan gave him drugs. When it got really bad I bought a cheap futon and put it on the floor next to his bed and slept there for a week until finally the pain was too much for either of us and Bob said, "Please." I asked Stan to do it. Tony and Donna stood with me with their hands on his warm fur when Stan put the needle in. I longed for my father's gentle hospice nurse to close his eyes.

I called Phillip. He cried on the phone. I told him when we got Bob's ashes back we were going to have a little service in the backyard before I closed on the house and he said if I didn't mind he'd like to come. He needed to pick up the rest of his stuff anyway. I said that was fine and that he should bring his girlfriend if he wanted. You can even stay here if you want I said. We wouldn't do that but thanks he said. And actually he said he'd been meaning to call and tell me. They'd gotten married a month ago. Good for you I said.

We held the service under the big oak tree. Stan and I, Donna and Nancy, Tony, Diane with Gregoire on a leash, Phillip and his hugely pregnant twenty-six-year-old wife Amanda all stood shivering in a circle in the frozen dirt and those of us who had known him told stories about Bob. Donna and Nancy held hands. Tony stood next to Amanda, who seemed confused, and explained to her what was going on. According to Tony, who summoned me to the garage later to fill me in while he had a smoke, Phillip hadn't mentioned they were attending a funeral for his dog or, for that matter, who I was. Amanda thought I was Phillip's cousin.

Afterward Martina stopped by with Gretchen. They had just adopted a shelter puppy and were picking up some of Bob's things, though I couldn't part with his collar and leash, which were richly impregnated with his sweet yeasty smell, or with a certain dear dirty toy in the shape of a bone with a face on each end.

Susan surprised everyone by flying in from Atlanta—she was on a book tour for *Daily Dispatches from the Edge of Beyond*. She arrived after it was over, all in black, in an airport limo with a raw steak in her Prada bag. She insisted we all put our coats back on and go out to watch as she laid the steak on Bob's grave and then tremulously recited the Twenty-Third Psalm. Gregoire licked the steak and when Susan went inside Stan cut it into slices for him. Donna and Nancy set out cookies and champagne in the dining room and Clement watched the proceedings from his perch on the kitchen counter.

I sold the house to a developer who knocked it down in one afternoon three weeks after I moved out, leaving a pile of rubble in the yard where Bob and Gregoire used to play stick. The plan, they told me at the closing, was to enlarge the footprint and build what they called a three-story six-bedroom luxury home with a gourmet kitchen, an attached four-car garage and an entertainment center in the basement.

I almost didn't care. By that time Stan, his dogs, Clement and I had moved into an old factory loft down the alley from the clinic. It had a roomy office for me and an extra bedroom for Gretchen who stayed with us sometimes on weekends when Martina, who was now in nursing school, studied for exams.

CHAPTER 64

Wei Chi / Before Completion

*The transition from chaos to order depends upon
your achieving true inner calm.*

It was spring again. It had rained every day for a week. The rain drew ancient essences out of the old brick and made the loft smell like the chemicals that once had been stored there. The rain streamed out of the gray sky not in drops but in sheets and seeped in around the metal casements in the filthy two-story windows. It was spring and it was cold and the windows needed replacing and the place needed airing and Clement needed to hunt. I'd kept him inside for as long as I could when we first moved to make sure he knew this was his new home, the place he should return to, and because we were in the city now. Though it was a quiet neighborhood I worried if his wits were a match for traffic and urban raccoons.

But one day, during a lull in the rain, he slipped out when I checked for the mail and didn't come back for three long days. I stood on the fire escape calling his name into the tunnel of the alley hoping for a flash of his luxuriant orange fur to appear around the edge of a garbage can. Stan set out a basket of dirty laundry hoping the smell of us would lure him home. He didn't appear and I thought I'd lost him. But on the third morning when he still hadn't shown up I looked out and saw, not Clement, but a familiar and comforting sight. There on the concrete step on the welcome mat at my new front door was the gift, neat and centered, one velvety gray mouse with praying hands, and I knew that we, despite all we'd lost, were home again.